Daily Quizzes
with Answer Key

(HOLT)

World History
The Human Journey

HOLT, RINEHART AND WINSTON
A Harcourt Education Company
Austin • Orlando • Chicago • New York • Toronto • London • San Diego

Cover description: Solyman II (1642–91)

Cover credit: John Young/Stapleton Collection, UK/Bridgeman

Copyright © by Holt, Rinehart and Winston

All rights reserved. No part of this publication may be reproduced or transmitted in any form or by any means, electronic or mechanical, including photocopy, recording, or any information storage and retrieval system, without permission in writing from the publisher.

Teachers using HOLT WORLD HISTORY: THE HUMAN JOURNEY may photocopy complete pages in sufficient quantities for classroom use only and not for resale.

Printed in the United States of America

ISBN 0-03-065739-3

3 4 5 6 7 8 9   054   05 04 03

Contents
Daily Quizzes

Unit 1 The Beginnings of Civilization

CHAPTER 1 The Emergence of Civilization
1 Prehistoric Peoples................1
2 The Foundations of Civilization.......2

CHAPTER 2 The First Civilizations
1 Ancient Kingdoms of the Nile........3
2 Egyptian Life and Culture..........4
3 Sumerian Civilization.............5
4 Empires of the Fertile Crescent.......6
5 The Phoenicians and the Lydians......7
6 The Origins of Judaism............8

CHAPTER 3 Ancient Indian Civilizations
1 Indus River Valley Civilization.......9
2 Indo-Aryan Migrants..............10
3 Hinduism and Buddhism...........11
4 Ancient Indian Dynasties and Empires....................12
5 Ancient Indian Life and Culture.....13

CHAPTER 4 Ancient Chinese Civilization
1 Geographic and Cultural Influences.....................14
2 The Shang Dynasty...............15
3 The Zhou, Qin, and Han Dynasties...16
4 Philosophies of Ancient China......17
5 Chinese Life and Culture...........18

Unit 2 The Growth of Civilizations

CHAPTER 5 The Greek City-States
1 Early Greeks and the Rise of City-States................19
2 Greek Government and Society......20
3 Sparta and Athens...............21
4 Daily Life in Athens..............22
5 The Expansion of Greece..........23

CHAPTER 6 Greece's Golden and Hellenistic Ages
1 Greek Art of the Golden Age........24
2 Philosophers and Writers of the Golden Age.................25
3 Alexander the Great..............26
4 The Spread of Hellenistic Culture.....27

CHAPTER 7 The Roman World
1 Founding the Roman Republic.......28
2 Rome Expands Its Borders..........29
3 The Birth of the Roman Empire......30
4 Roman Society and Culture.........31
5 The Rise of Christianity............32
6 The Fall of the Western Empire......33

CHAPTER 8 Africa
1 Africa's Early History..............34
2 The Kingdoms of Kush and Aksum...35
3 Trading States of Africa............36

CHAPTER 9 The Americas
1 The Earliest Americans............37
2 Cultures of North America.........38
3 Mesoamerica and Andean South America..................39

Unit 3 (Modern Unit 1) The World in Transition

CHAPTER 10 (Modern CHAPTER 1) The Byzantine Empire and Russia
1 The Byzantine Empire.............40
2 The Rise of Russia................41
3 Russia and the Mongols...........42

CHAPTER 11 (Modern CHAPTER 2) The Islamic World
1 The Rise of Islam................43
2 The Spread of Islam..............44
3 Islamic Civilization...............45

CHAPTER 12 (Modern CHAPTER 3) The Civilizations of East Asia
1 China under the Sui, Tang, and Sung Dynasties..............46
2 The Mongol Empire..............47
3 Japan, Korea, and Southeast Asia.....48

CHAPTER 13 (Modern CHAPTER 4) The Rise of the Middle Ages
1 The Rise of the Franks.............49
2 Feudalism and the Manorial System................50
3 The Church......................51
4 The Struggle for Power in England and France..............52
5 The Clash Over Germany and Italy......................53

Contents

Daily Quizzes

CHAPTER 14 (Modern CHAPTER 5)
The High Middle Ages
1. The Crusades 54
2. The Revival of Trade 55
3. The Growth of Towns 56
4. Life and Culture in the Middle Ages 57
5. Wars and the Growth of Nations 58
6. Challenges to Church Power 59

Unit 4 (Modern Unit 2) The Age of Exploration and Expansion

CHAPTER 15 (Modern CHAPTER 6)
The Renaissance and Reformation
1. The Italian Renaissance 60
2. The Northern Renaissance 61
3. The Protestant Reformation 62
4. The Catholic Reformation 63
5. Culture and Daily Life 64

CHAPTER 16 (Modern CHAPTER 7)
Exploration and Expansion
1. The Scientific Revolution 65
2. The Foundations of European Exploration 66
3. Voyages of Portugal and Spain 67
4. The Spanish and Dutch Empires 68

CHAPTER 17 (Modern CHAPTER 8)
Asia in Transition
1. The Ming and Qing Dynasties 69
2. China and Europeans 70
3. The Tokugawa Shoguns in Japan 71

CHAPTER 18 (Modern CHAPTER 9)
Islamic Empires in Asia
1. The Ottoman Empire 72
2. The Safavid Empire 73
3. The Mughal Empire in India 74

Unit 5 (Modern Unit 3) From Absolutism to Revolution

CHAPTER 19 (Modern CHAPTER 10)
Monarchs of Europe
1. France in the Age of Absolutism 75
2. Russia in the Age of Absolutism 76
3. Central Europe in the Age of Absolutism 77
4. The English Monarchy 78

Chapter 20 (Modern CHAPTER 11)
Enlightenment and Revolution in England and America
1. Civil War and Revolution 79
2. Constitutional Monarchy in England 80
3. English Colonial Expansion 81
4. The Enlightenment 82
5. The American Revolution 83

CHAPTER 21 (Modern CHAPTER 12)
The French Revolution and Napoléon
1. The Roots of Revolution 84
2. The French Revolution 85
3. The French Republic 86
4. The Napoléonic Era 87
5. A Return to Peace 88

Unit 6 (Modern Unit 4) Industrialization and Nationalism

CHAPTER 22 (Modern CHAPTER 13)
The Industrial Revolution
1. Origins of the Industrial Revolution 89
2. The Factory System 90
3. New Methods and Business Organizations 91
4. Living and Working Conditions 92
5. Socialism 93

Contents
Daily Quizzes

CHAPTER 23 (Modern Chapter 14)
Life in the Industrial Age
1 Advances in Technology and Communication 94
2 Advances in Science and Medicine 95
3 Social Sciences in the Industrial Age 96
4 Society and Culture in the Industrial Age 97
5 Literature, Music, and Art in the Industrial Age 98

CHAPTER 24 (Modern CHAPTER 15)
The Age of Reform
1 Liberal Reforms in Great Britain and Its Empire 99
2 Expansion and Reform in the United States 100
3 Revolution and Reform in France 101
4 Latin Americans Win Independence 102

CHAPTER 25 (Modern Chapter 16)
Nationalism in Europe
1 The Unification of Italy 103
2 The Unification of Germany 104
3 Opposition to Bismarck 105
4 Reform and Revolution in Russia 106
5 Unrest in Austria-Hungary 107

CHAPTER 26 (Modern CHAPTER 17)
The Age of Imperialism
1 The Roots of Western Imperialism 108
2 European Claims in North Africa 109
3 European Claims in Sub-Saharan Africa 110
4 Expansion in Asia 111
5 Imperialism in Latin America 112

Unit 7 (Modern Unit 5)
World War in the Twentieth Century

CHAPTER 27 (Modern CHAPTER 18)
World War I and the Russian Revolution
1 Setting the Stage for War 113
2 World War I: A New Kind of War 114
3 The Russian Revolution 115
4 The Terms of Peace 116
5 Creating a "New" Europe 117

CHAPTER 28 (Modern CHAPTER 19)
The Great Depression and the Rise of Totalitarianism
1 The Postwar Era 118
2 Postwar Prosperity Crumbles 119
3 Political Tensions After World War I 120
4 Fascist Dictatorships in Italy and Germany 121
5 Dictatorship in the Soviet Union 122

CHAPTER 29 (Modern CHAPTER 20)
Nationalist Movements Around the World
1 The British Empire in the Postwar Era 123
2 Turkey, Persia, and Africa 124
3 Unrest in China 125
4 Imperialism in Japan 126
5 Latin America Between the Wars 127

CHAPTER 30 (Modern CHAPTER 21)
World War II
1 Threats to World Peace 128
2 Hitler's Aggressions 129
3 Axis Gains 130
4 The Soviet Union and the United States 131
5 The Holocaust 132
6 The End of the War 133

Contents
Daily Quizzes

Unit 8 (Modern Unit 6)
The World Since 1945

Chapter 31 (Modern CHAPTER 22)
Europe and North America in the Postwar Years
1. Aftermath of the War in Europe 134
2. Origins of the Cold War 135
3. Reconstruction, Reform, and Reaction in Europe 136
4. The United States and Canada 137

CHAPTER 32 (Modern CHAPTER 23)
Asia Since 1945
1. South Asia After Empire 138
2. Communist China and Its Influence 139
3. The Japanese Miracle 140
4. Independence Struggles in Southeast Asia 141
5. Asian Paths to Prosperity 142

CHAPTER 33 (Modern CHAPTER 24)
Africa and Middle East Since 1945
1. African Independence After World War II 143
2. Africa Since Independence 144
3. Nationalism in the Middle East and North Africa 145
4. War, Revolution, and Oil in the Middle East and North Africa 146

CHAPTER 34 (Modern CHAPTER 25)
Latin America Since 1945
1. Facing New Challenges 147
2. Mexico and Central America 148
3. Nations of the Caribbean 149
4. South America 150

CHAPTER 35 (Modern CHAPTER 26)
The Superpowers in the Modern Era
1. The Industrial Powers of North America 151
2. Europe 152
3. The Fall of Communism 153
4. A Day That Changed the World 154

CHAPTER 36 (Modern CHAPTER 27)
The Modern World
1. The Arts and Literature 155
2. Science and Technology 156
3. Human Rights and the Spread of Democratic Ideals 157

EPILOGUE: The Modern World
1. Revolution to Imperialism 158
2. World War in the Twentieth Century 159
3. Europe and the Americas Since 1945 160
4. Asia, Africa, and the Middle East Since 1945 161
5. The Modern Era and Beyond 162
6. A Day That Changed the World 163

PROLOGUE: The Ancient World
1. The First Civilizations 164
2. Ancient India and China 165
3. Civilizations of the Mediterranean World 166
4. Africa and the Americas 167

ANSWER KEY 168

Name _____ Class _____ Date _____

Daily Quiz 1.1
Prehistoric Peoples

MATCHING *(10 points each)* Match each of the following people or terms with the correct description by writing the letter of the description in the space provided. Some descriptions will not be used.

_____ 1. hominids

_____ 2. *Homo sapiens*

_____ 3. Ice Age

_____ 4. Neanderthals

_____ 5. Cro-Magnons

_____ 6. Mesolithic Age

_____ 7. agriculture

_____ 8. Neolithic Age

_____ 9. hunter-gatherers

_____ 10. Neolithic agricultural revolution

a. period when humans began to settle in villages, developed agriculture, and domesticated animals

b. period when humans made fishing tools, bows and arrows, tamed dogs

c. raising of crops for food

d. period when the cold climate helped create landbridges

e. societies in which some people caught animals for food while others looked for plants and fruit

f. oldest stone age

g. wore animal skin for clothing, used fire, buried their dead

h. any ancient human or humanlike creature

i. process when people began to develop ways to produce their own food

j. tools, clothing, works of art, weapons, and toys of a culture

k. improved tools and weapons and painted stories on cave walls

l. All modern people are part of this species.

Name _____ Class _____ Date _____

CHAPTER 1

Daily Quiz 1.2

The Foundations of Civilization

TRUE/FALSE *(10 points each)* Mark each statement *T* if it is true or *F* if it is false. If false explain why.

_____ 1. Hunting and gathering societies advanced more rapidly than agricultural settlements.

_____ 2. Irrigation was developed so farmers could make it through dry seasons.

_____ 3. Governments were created to help make rules for human behavior.

_____ 4. Artisans made their living by buying and selling goods.

_____ 5. The spread of ideas from one area to another is called division of culture.

_____ 6. Calendars were based on the phases of the moon.

_____ 7. Writing was developed in order to help people communicate.

_____ 8. Bronze tools were more advanced than tools made from iron.

_____ 9. The invention of the plow made women the most important people in agricultural societies.

_____ 10. Religious beliefs had little effect on early human civilizations.

Daily Quiz 2.1

Ancient Kingdoms of the Nile

FILL IN THE BLANK *(10 points each)* For each of the following statements, fill in the blank with the appropriate word, phrase, or name.

1. People were able to settle in ancient Egypt because the _____ helped support farming.

2. Farmers coped with the yearly floods by creating systems of _____.

3. The Nile Valley protected Egyptians from invaders because it was surrounded by _____.

4. Egyptians developed _____ to help communicate and record history.

5. The _____ provided the key to hieroglyphics because it also contained Greek text.

6. The Great Sphinx and the largest pyramids were built during the period known as the _____.

7. Civil wars divided Egypt when the _____ became stronger than the pharaohs.

8. The Hyksos, or _____, took over parts of Egypt after the collapse of the Middle Kingdom.

9. _____ was a female pharoah who ruled during the New Kingdom.

10. Amenhotep IV tried to convert Egypt to _____.

Name _____ Class _____ Date _____

Daily Quiz 2.2
Egyptian Life and Culture

MULTIPLE CHOICE *(10 points each)* For each of the following, write the letter of the best choice in the space provided.

_____ 1. Egyptian civilization survived for centuries because the
   a. dynasties provided a stable government.
   b. geography of the Nile Valley provided food and protection.
   c. priests and nobles helped keep the peace.
   d. pyramids offered protection from invaders.

_____ 2. Egyptian engineers may have used ramps and levers to
   a. build the pyramids.
   b. create lifelike statues.
   c. irrigate their fields.
   d. protect the pharaohs.

_____ 3. Egyptians kept track of years by
   a. counting the years of a pharaoh's reign.
   b. counting five extra days on the calendar.
   c. the time of the harvest.
   d. the time spent on building a pyramid.

_____ 4. Scribes were valuable because they could
   a. design pyramids.
   b. use stars to create calendars.
   c. read and write.
   d. treat illnesses.

_____ 5. At first, Egyptians believed that life after death
   a. was only for animals.
   b. was like life on Earth.
   c. did not exist.
   d. was only for pharaohs.

_____ 6. Egyptians used chemicals to
   a. preserve bodies after death.
   b. improve farming.
   c. create materials to build pyramids.
   d. anoint the pharaohs.

_____ 7. Egyptian women
   a. did most of the farming.
   b. had no rights.
   c. were allowed to own and inherit property.
   d. were able to move from the lower to the upper class.

_____ 8. Peasants were allowed to
   a. keep all of their crops.
   b. keep none of their crops.
   c. keep some of their crops.
   d. become upper-class citizens.

_____ 9. Caravans were used by
   a. soldiers.
   b. merchants and traders.
   c. farmers.
   d. the pharaohs.

_____ 10. Egyptian merchants and traders helped
   a. improve the lives of peasants.
   b. keep the pharaohs in power.
   c. supply the army.
   d. spread Egyptian culture.

Name _____ Class _____ Date _____

Daily Quiz 2.3

Sumerian Civilization

TRUE/FALSE Mark each statement *T* if it is true or *F* if it is false. If false explain why.

_____ 1. Like Egypt, the geography of the Fertile Crescent protected it from invaders.
_____

_____ 2. Neolithic farmers formed a society because they needed to cooperate to irrigate the land.
_____

_____ 3. The predictable flood patterns of the Tigris and Euphrates rivers made farming easier.
_____

_____ 4. Like the Egyptians, Sumerians used a picture-based form of writing called hieroglyphics.
_____

_____ 5. Sumerian buildings were weakened by their use of the arch.
_____

_____ 6. The Sumerians created a number system based on 60.
_____

_____ 7. The Sumerians believed that their city-states belonged to the people who lived in them.
_____

_____ 8. Sumerians grew enough food to allow for a division of labor.
_____

_____ 9. All upper-class Sumerians received an education.
_____

_____ 10. The Sumerians did not believe in an afterlife.
_____

Name _____ Class _____ Date _____

Daily Quiz 2.4
Empires of the Fertile Crescent

MATCHING *(10 points each)* In the space provided, write the letter of the term or place that matches each description. Some answers will not be used.

_____ 1. Akkadians

_____ 2. Sargon

_____ 3. Hammurabi

_____ 4. Code of Hammurabi

_____ 5. Babylonians

_____ 6. Hittites

_____ 7. Assyrians

_____ 8. *Epic of Gilgamesh*

_____ 9. Nebuchadnezzar

_____ 10. Cyrus

a. religious practices of these people focused on success on Earth, rather than preparation for afterlife

b. capital city during Assyrian rule

c. had a code of laws in which only major crimes received the death penalty

d. spoke a language related to modern Arabic and Hebrew

e. Babylonian leader who conquered most of the Tigris-Euphrates Valley

f. Persian king who failed to conquer Greece

g. Persian king who conquered Babylon and most of Asia Minor

h. invaders who were the first to use soldiers on horseback

i. laws in which punishment was based on the concept of an "eye for an eye"

j. one of the oldest works of literature

k. Chaldean leader who returned Babylon to power and wealth

l. powerful Akkadian king

m. one of the Seven Wonders of the World

Name _____ Class _____ Date _____

 Daily Quiz 2.5

The Phoenicians and the Lydians

SHORT ANSWER *(10 points each)* Use the space provided to answer the following questions.

1. Why was it difficult for the Phoenicians to migrate to the east? _____
_____

2. How did the Phoenicians conduct most of their trade? _____
_____

3. Name one of the places where the Phoenicians had colonies. _____
_____

4. What was the Phoenicians' most important natural resource? _____
_____

5. Name two important Phoenician exports. _____
_____

6. What cultures did the Phoenicians imitate? _____
_____

7. What does it mean to barter? _____
_____

8. What was the Phoenicians' most important contribution to the world? _____
_____

9. What are the Lydians most famous for? _____
_____

10. What is a money economy? _____
_____

Copyright © by Holt, Rinehart and Winston. All rights reserved.

Name _____ Class _____ Date _____

Daily Quiz 2.6

The Origins of Judaism

MULTIPLE CHOICE *(10 points each)* For each of the following, write the letter of the best choice in the space provided.

_____ 1. According to the Bible, Jacob's sons established the
   a. Twelve Tribes of Israel.
   b. land of Canaan.
   c. Twelve Tribes of Abraham.
   d. Twelve Tribes of Hebrew.

_____ 2. The Exodus, or the Hebrew's flight from Egypt, occurred because
   a. the Hyksos had invaded Egypt.
   b. Moses had invaded Egypt.
   c. the Egyptians had enslaved the Hebrews.
   d. the Egyptians had enslaved the Hyksos.

_____ 3. The Ten Commandments were
   a. the rules for a democracy.
   b. the rules the Canaanites followed in Egypt.
   c. a set of moral laws.
   d. the rules for a money economy.

_____ 4. Moses told the Hebrews to settle in the promised land, which was
   a. Philistine.
   b. Canaan.
   c. the Sinai Peninsula.
   d. Egypt.

_____ 5. In Canaan, the Hebrew tribes were united under
   a. King David.
   b. King Canaan.
   c. Moses.
   d. King Saul.

_____ 6. King David established the tradition of kings making a covenant with
   a. the Bible.
   b. nearby kingdoms.
   c. God and the people.
   d. Eygpt.

_____ 7. After King Solomon's death, Israel split into two parts named
   a. Israel and Judah.
   b. Samaria and Judah.
   c. Samaria and Jerusalem.
   d. Israel and Jerusalem.

_____ 8. Mosaic law placed a specific emphasis on
   a. "an eye for an eye."
   b. kindness and respect for all people.
   c. honoring priests and kings.
   d. believing the prophets' messages.

_____ 9. The Hebrews believed that Yahweh
   a. chose the people's destinies.
   b. allowed people to choose between good and evil.
   c. allowed people to live without fear of punishment.
   d. chose those who were good and those who were bad.

_____ 10. Judeo-Christian ethics emphasizes
   a. proper behavior.
   b. crimes and punishment.
   c. ways to worship God.
   d. money.

Name _____ Class _____ Date _____

Daily Quiz 3.1
Indus River Valley Civilization

MATCHING *(10 points each)* In the space provided, write the letter of the term or place that matches each description. Some answers will not be used.

_____ 1. Indian subcontinent

_____ 2. Himalayas

_____ 3. Khyber Pass

_____ 4. Indo-Gangetic Plain

_____ 5. the Deccan

_____ 6. monsoon

_____ 7. southwest monsoon

_____ 8. Harappan

_____ 9. citadel

_____ 10. Mohenjo Daro

a. brings the rainy season

b. path crossing the mountains into India

c. plateau with mild summer climate

d. extends southward from central Asia to the Indian Ocean

e. region drained by the Ganges and Indus Rivers

f. fortress built on a brick platform

g. mountain range on the Arabian Sea

h. ancient civilization in the Indus River valley

i. separates India from the rest of Asia

j. ancient Harrapan city

k. winds that mark the seasons in India

l. possible religious or ceremonial location

Name _____ Class _____ Date _____

CHAPTER 3

Daily Quiz 3.2
Indo-Aryan Migrants

MULTIPLE CHOICE *(10 points each)* For each of the following, write the letter of the best choice in the space provided.

_____ 1. Indo-Aryans came from
  a. northwestern India.
  b. Harappa.
  c. the Hindu-Kush Mountains.
  d. north of the Black and Caspian Seas.

_____ 2. The Vedas were the
  a. Indo-Aryan army.
  b. Indo-Aryan word for war.
  c. Indo-Aryans' works of religious literature.
  d. Indo-Aryan form of writing.

_____ 3. Indo-Aryan gods were based on
  a. a spiritual force.
  b. super humans.
  c. nature.
  d. priests and kings.

_____ 4. In Indo-Aryan society, Brahmins were
  a. special priests.
  b. kings.
  c. soldiers.
  d. peasants.

_____ 5. Indo-Aryan states were ruled by
  a. rajas.
  b. the people.
  c. priests.
  d. warriors.

_____ 6. Indo-Aryans placed a high value on
  a. trade.
  b. marriage.
  c. nomadic life.
  d. building.

_____ 7. Indo-Aryans spoke
  a. Harappa.
  b. Vedas.
  c. Indian.
  d. Sanskrit.

_____ 8. Indo-Aryans enforced rigid
  a. trading laws.
  b. social classes.
  c. money exchange laws.
  d. migration laws.

_____ 9. Indo-Aryan migrants had the most significant impact on
  a. northern India.
  b. southern India.
  c. the coastal plains.
  d. Himalayan societies.

_____ 10. Rough terrain in southern India prevented
  a. farming.
  b. the unification of its peoples.
  c. wars.
  d. the development of agriculture.

Copyright © by Holt, Rinehart and Winston. All rights reserved.

Name _____ Class _____ Date _____

Daily Quiz 3.3
Hinduism and Buddhism

MATCHING *(10 points each)* In the space provided, write the letter of the term or place that matches each description. Some answers will not be used.

_____ 1. Upanishads
_____ 2. Ramayana
_____ 3. caste system
_____ 4. varnas
_____ 5. Pariahs
_____ 6. monism
_____ 7. maya
_____ 8. Siddhartha Gautama
_____ 9. Right Intentions
_____ 10. Mahayana Buddhism

a. system of social organization
b. the "untouchables"
c. belief that the world was an illusion
d. belief that God and creation are the same
e. Indian name for social classes
f. epic poem that explained the ideas of Vedanta
g. living a life of good will; striving toward perfection
h. doing one's moral duty in life
i. belief that Buddha was a god
j. mental and physical practices that bring the body and mind together
k. Buddha
l. written explanations of the Vedic religion
m. search for truth and meaning

Name _____ Class _____ Date _____

CHAPTER 3

Daily Quiz 3.4

Ancient Indian Dynasties and Empires

FILL IN THE BLANK *(10 points each)* For each of the following statements, fill in the blank with the appropriate word, phrase, or name.

1. The unification of India helped to protect it from _____.

2. Darius the Great and the Persian Empire invaded and ruled the Indus River valley until it was defeated by _____.

3. Northern and northwestern India were conquered by _____.

4. Chandragupta Maurya used a _____ to carry out his commands.

5. Except for the southern tip, all of India was united under _____.

6. The Mauryan ruler Aśoka, sick of killing, became a _____.

7. During his reign, Aśoka worked to improve _____.

8. The Mauryan Empire began to decline because of _____.

9. The dominant religion during the Gupta dynasty was _____.

10. The Gupta political system gave power to _____.

Name _____ Class _____ Date _____

Daily Quiz 3.5

Ancient Indian Life and Culture

TRUE/FALSE Mark each statement *T* if it is true or *F* if it is false. If false explain why.

_____ 1. Peasants in northern India had to give up portions of their crops to their rulers.

_____ 2. Southern India's economy relied on international trade.

_____ 3. The Hindu Laws of Manu granted women the same rights as men.

_____ 4. Suttee was the practice of having more than one wife.

_____ 5. The *Panchatantra* explained the Hindu laws of Manu.

_____ 6. Indian drama developed during the Gupta period.

_____ 7. The great Mauryan ruler Aśoka forbade all symbols of Buddhism, including stupas.

_____ 8. In ancient India, children of all castes were able to study the great epic poems and mathematics.

_____ 9. Aryabhata was a famous Indian mathematician.

_____ 10. Indian doctors developed inoculations to help with plastic surgery.

CHAPTER 4

Daily Quiz 4.1
Geographic and Cultural Influences

FILL IN THE BLANK *(10 points each)* For each of the following statements, fill in the blank with the appropriate word, phrase, or name.

1. Plentiful rain in central and southern China makes _____ the main crop.

2. The Huang, Chang, and Xi are the great rivers found in China _____.

3. _____ is one of the regions that surrounds the heart of China.

4. The _____ in the Huang River valley washes into the Huang River and tints it yellow.

5. Because of its disastrous flooding, the Huang has been nicknamed "China's _____."

6. _____ built to prevent flooding from the Huang have actually made the problem worse.

7. The great rivers of China are important to the economy because they can be used as _____.

8. Geographical features such as mountains and _____ isolated China from other cultures.

9. China's isolation gave its people a strong sense of _____.

10. China called itself *Zhongguo*, which means the _____.

Name _____ Class _____ Date _____

Daily Quiz 4.2
The Shang Dynasty

MULTIPLE CHOICE *(10 points each)* For each of the following, write the letter of the best choice in the space provided.

_____ 1. According to Chinese legend, Yu established a line of kings called the
   a. Pangu.
   b. Xia.
   c. Shang.
   d. Huang.

_____ 2. The first historic dynasty in China was the
   a. Shang.
   b. Tang.
   c. Xia.
   d. Chang.

_____ 3. The Shang probably gained control of the Huang River valley because they
   a. resisted invaders.
   b. threatened the people.
   c. improved farming.
   d. could manage irrigation and flooding in the valley.

_____ 4. The Shang were able to gain territory and influence other regions because of
   a. their control of the Huang River valley.
   b. a simple government.
   c. instability caused by nomadic warriors.
   d. a complex government and strong military.

_____ 5. Shang pottery is distinctive because of its use of
   a. silk.
   b. bone.
   c. kaolin.
   d. jade.

_____ 6. The Shang government managed the lunar calendar by employing
   a. astronomers.
   b. priests.
   c. priest-astronomers.
   d. farmers.

_____ 7. The religion that developed during the Shang period was a combination of ancestor worship and
   a. monotheism.
   b. animism.
   c. reincarnation.
   d. nirvana.

_____ 8. The Chinese developed a written language that could be used by people who spoke any
   a. dialect.
   b. language.
   c. accent.
   d. ideograph.

_____ 9. During the Shang period, writing became an art called
   a. pictography.
   b. calligraphy.
   c. scripting.
   d. painting.

_____ 10. The Shang dynasty fell because
   a. it was unfit to rule.
   b. it could not protect its borders.
   c. the last Shang ruler died.
   d. it did not develop an economy.

Name _____ Class _____ Date _____

CHAPTER 4  Daily Quiz 4.3

The Zhou, Qin, and Han Dynasties

TRUE/FALSE Mark each statement *T* if it is true or *F* if it is false. If false explain why.

_____ 1. After their conquest of the Shang, the Zhou formed a strong central government.

_____ 2. The Zhou dynasty fell because of infighting among local leaders, as well as outside attacks.

_____ 3. The Qin dynasty established a democracy to give the people a voice.

_____ 4. Cheng, the Qin emperor, believed in freedom of expression.

_____ 5. The Qin protected themselves with bands of patrolling warriors along their borders.

_____ 6. The Qin dynasty angered the public by using enforced labor for public works.

_____ 7. The Han dynasty lost territory, and China's borders receded during Han reign.

_____ 8. The Han dynasty created a civil service to run the government.

_____ 9. The Han emperor Liu Ch'e allowed prices to run out of control, a practice that hurt the peasants.

_____ 10. The Han dynasty prospered because of trade along the Huang River.

Daily Quiz 4.4
Philosophies of Ancient China

MATCHING *(10 points each)* In the space provided, write the letter of the term or place that matches each description. Some answers will not be used.

_____ 1. dualism

_____ 2. yin

_____ 3. yang

_____ 4. Confucius

_____ 5. *Analects*

_____ 6. Confucianism

_____ 7. Daoism

_____ 8. Laozi

_____ 9. Legalism

_____ 10. Buddhism

a. belief that people were by nature selfish and untrustworthy and needed harsh laws

b. religion that became popular during turbulent times

c. bright, active force

d. philosopher who sought to end political disorder

e. belief in the importance of family, respect for elders, reverence for past

f. belief that the way to harmony is an understanding of nature

g. dark, passive force

h. book of Laozi's teachings

i. belief in the two-sidedness of nature

j. founded Daoism

k. writings that contained the ideas of Confucius

l. dynasty whose rule was guided by Legalism

Name _____ Class _____ Date _____

CHAPTER  Daily Quiz 4.5
Chinese Life and Culture

FILL IN THE BLANK *(10 points each)* For each of the following statements, fill in the blank with the appropriate word, phrase, or name.

1. The Chinese believed that the well-being of the state relied on the strength of the _____.

2. In Chinese society, family was more important than the _____.

3. Chinese families kept detailed family records, known as a _____.

4. Chinese respect for the family included respect for the past and for _____.

5. The most important member of a Chinese family was the _____.

6. Trade was less important than farming until the _____.

7. Chinese education was based on the study of _____.

8. _____ is the text that teaches manners and ceremonies.

9. The Chinese invented the _____ to help prepare them for earthquakes.

10. The Daoist belief in the body's life force energy is the basis for _____.

Copyright © by Holt, Rinehart and Winston. All rights reserved.
World History: The Human Journey

Name _____ Class _____ Date _____

Daily Quiz 5.1

Early Greeks and the Rise of City-States

TRUE/FALSE *(10 points each)* Mark each statement *T* if it is true or *F* if it is false. If false explain why.

_____ 1. The Greek mainland is bordered by the Atlantic Ocean.

_____ 2. Geographical features of Greece encouraged the formation of larger villages.

_____ 3. The Minoan was the earliest known Greek civilization.

_____ 4. Minoan civilization weakened because it failed to establish a strong navy.

_____ 5. Mycenaean society was ruled by warrior leaders of clans and tribes.

_____ 6. The warring attitudes of the Mycenaeans brought down advances made by the Minoans.

_____ 7. Greek civilization was based around the polis, or agriculture.

_____ 8. Greek city-states usually included an agora, or marketplace.

_____ 9. In Greek city-states, all people were citizens.

_____ 10. Greek city-states shared a language and religious beliefs.

Name _____ Class _____ Date _____

Daily Quiz 5.2
Greek Government and Society

MULTIPLE CHOICE *(10 points each)* For each of the following, write the letter of the best choice in the space provided.

_____ 1. The *Iliad* and the *Odyssey* are both long poems about heroes and are known as
   a. ballads.
   b. epics.
   c. agoras.
   d. cuneiform.

_____ 2. The *Iliad* tells the story of the
   a. Trojan War.
   b. Hellenic War.
   c. Mycenaen War.
   d. Paris War.

_____ 3. Because of the poem by Homer, the word *odyssey* now means
   a. soldier-king.
   b. Greek Island.
   c. long, adventure-filled journey.
   d. great victory.

_____ 4. Greek religion sought to explain nature and
   a. emotions.
   b. medicine.
   c. war.
   d. the afterlife.

_____ 5. Greeks called the stories that explained their world and religion
   a. myths.
   b. legends.
   c. fables.
   d. fairy tales.

_____ 6. Greeks believed that oracles could
   a. help them win battles.
   b. tell them about the future.
   c. help them gain riches.
   d. help them grow better crops.

_____ 7. The Greeks believed that athletic contests such as the Olympics
   a. protected them from invaders.
   b. helped them in the afterlife.
   c. prepared them for war.
   d. pleased the gods.

_____ 8. City-states controlled by wealthy Greek nobles were known as
   a. polis.
   b. Olympians.
   c. aristocracies.
   d. acropolis.

_____ 9. Wealthy people eventually brought down the noble class with a hired army called the
   a. aristocrats.
   b. cavalry.
   c. hoplites.
   d. tyrants.

_____ 10. Greek city-states began to form governments ruled by the people, or by
   a. cities.
   b. aristocracies.
   c. tyrants.
   d. democracies.

Copyright © by Holt, Rinehart and Winston. All rights reserved.

Daily Quiz 5.3

Sparta and Athens

FILL IN THE BLANK *(10 points each)* For each of the following statements, fill in the blank with the appropriate word, phrase, or name.

1. Invaders from the north conquered the Peloponnesians and made them into slaves, or _____.

2. In Spartan society, half-citizens were free but had no _____.

3. The Spartan assembly elected five _____, who made sure the king acted within the law.

4. Spartan military society was strong, but there was little _____.

5. All Athenian men were citizens, regardless of rank or _____.

6. Metics were people who _____.

7. All male Athenians served in the assembly, where they annually elected nine rulers, or _____.

8. _____ ended the practice of becoming slaves to pay debts.

9. _____ turned Athens into a direct democracy.

10. A direct democracy means all _____.

Name _____ Class _____ Date _____

Daily Quiz 5.4

Daily Life in Athens

SHORT ANSWER *(10 points each)* Use the space provided to answer the following questions.

1. How did the Athenians spread their culture around the Mediterranean? _____

2. How did Athenians feel about spending money on buildings? _____

3. What was the purpose of marriage, according to the Athenians? _____

4. What kind of legal and social rights did Athenian women have? _____

5. What famous Greek poet wrote about everyday life in Athens? _____

6. What was a pedagogue? _____

7. What did the phrase "a sound mind in a healthy body" say about Athenian education? _____

8. Sophists ran schools for older boys. What does the word *sophos* mean? _____

9. What is the study of ethics? _____

10. What is the study of rhetoric? _____

Name _____ Class _____ Date _____

Daily Quiz 5.5

The Expansion of Greece

MULTIPLE CHOICE *(10 points each)* For each of the following, write the letter of the best choice in the space provided.

_____ 1. The Persian Wars began when
  a. the Persians invaded Athens.
  b. Greek colonies rebelled against Persian rule.
  c. Greece invaded Persia.
  d. Persian colonies rebelled against Athenian rule.

_____ 2. Outnumbered Athenians turned back Persian invaders at the
  a. Battle of Marathon.
  b. Battle of Macedonia.
  c. Battle of Darius.
  d. Battle of Thrace.

_____ 3. Spartan fighters at the Battle of Thermopylae
  a. gave other Greek city-states time to prepare to fight.
  b. defeated the Persians, even though they were badly outnumbered.
  c. defeated the Athenians.
  d. joined the Persians and turned against Athens.

_____ 4. The Greeks defeated the Persians in a sea battle led by
  a. Sparta.
  b. Xerxes.
  c. Themistocles.
  d. Thermopylae.

_____ 5. The Persian Wars helped the Greek city-states
  a. become more self-sufficient.
  b. build better forts.
  c. develop trade with Persia.
  d. unify to protect themselves.

_____ 6. The Delian League was a
  a. league of Athenian colonies.
  b. group of city-states that had trade agreements.
  c. league that gave rights to Greek slaves.
  d. league of city-states united to protect themselves.

_____ 7. During Pericles' rule, public office could be held by
  a. all landowners.
  b. military officers only.
  c. free men and women.
  d. all free men.

_____ 8. Under Pericles, Athens gained power while other Delian League states
  a. weakened.
  b. also grew stronger.
  c. joined with Persia.
  d. became direct democracies.

_____ 9. The Peloponnesian War broke out when
  a. Pericles died.
  b. tension between Athens and Sparta boiled over
  c. Persia invaded Peloponnesus.
  d. Persia invaded Athens.

_____ 10. The Peloponnesian War lasted until the Spartans
  a. joined with Syracuse to cut off Athens' food supply.
  b. were depleted by plague.
  c. joined with Persia to cut off Athens' food supply.
  d. defeated Athens at Syracuse.

Name _____ Class _____ Date _____

 Daily Quiz 6.1

Greek Art of the Golden Age

FILL IN THE BLANK *(10 points each)* For each of the following statements, fill in the blank with the appropriate word, phrase, or name.

1. Athens was the center of culture during the _____ of Greece.

2. Athenian culture placed a high value on _____, which showed in their art and architecture.

3. Athens' center was a high hill called the _____.

4. Athenians built a temple named the _____ to the goddess Athena.

5. Surviving Greek paintings show an emphasis on realism by depicting scenes from _____.

6. Greek sculptures were stiff and structured at first, but later they began to look _____.

7. Phidias made large formal sculptures, such as the statue of _____, one of the Seven Wonders of the World.

8. Greek art not only glorified the gods, but also showed admiration for _____ beauty.

9. The Greeks' art showed pride in their _____.

10. Greek art was meant to express a belief in balance, or _____.

Name _____ Class _____ Date _____

Daily Quiz 6.2

Philosophers and Writers of the Golden Age

MATCHING *(10 points each)* Match each of the following people or terms with the correct description by writing the letter of the description in the space provided. Some descriptions will not be used.

_____ 1. philosophy

_____ 2. cosmologists

_____ 3. Socrates

_____ 4. Socratic Method

_____ 5. Plato

_____ 6. Aristotle

_____ 7. Hippocrates

_____ 8. Thucydides

_____ 9. tragedies

_____ 10. Euripides

a. trained doctors to base medical treatment on reason, not magic

b. realistic playwright who wrote *The Trojan Women*, showing the misery of war

c. taught that education led to personal growth

d. teaching through questioning

e. plays where the hero was punished for pride or defeated by outside forces

f. imaginary discussions among several people

g. believed that humans could not reach perfection

h. theory that all things in the world are imperfect versions of a perfect idea

i. developed atomic theory through use of logic and mathematics

j. study of basic questions of reality and human existence

k. believed that knowledge could only be gained through logical study

l. government combining monarchy, aristocracy, and democracy

m. those who tried to understand the nature of the physical universe

n. believed that studying the past helps us understand human nature

Name _____ Class _____ Date _____

CHAPTER 6

Daily Quiz 6.3
Alexander the Great

MULTIPLE CHOICE *(10 points each)* For each of the following, write the letter of the best choice in the space provided.

_____ 1. Philip II of Macedon gained power by
   a. recruiting his own army.
   b. borrowing from nobles.
   c. inheriting an army.
   d. inheriting a throne.

_____ 2. Philip's army used the Greek idea of a phalanx, which was
   a. an 18-foot spear.
   b. a cavalry charge.
   c. soldiers scattering to attack from all angles.
   d. soldiers marching shoulder to shoulder in tight rows.

_____ 3. An uprising against Philip's rule was organized by
   a. Euripides.
   b. Socrates.
   c. Persia.
   d. Demosthenes.

_____ 4. Philip's son Alexander was ready to lead because he
   a. fought battles before age 20.
   b. had both classical and military training.
   c. trained with the Spartan army.
   d. studied with Socrates.

_____ 5. Alexander's ultimate goal was to conquer
   a. Persia.
   b. Sparta.
   c. all of the known world.
   d. Greek city-states.

_____ 6. Alexander's plans fell short several times because
   a. his troops rebelled or died.
   b. the Persians fought back.
   c. the Indians fought back.
   d. he could not cross rivers.

_____ 7. Through his conquests, Alexander hoped to
   a. bring slaves to Greece.
   b. create a greater army.
   c. spread Greek culture.
   d. absorb Persian culture.

_____ 8. Alexander kept his empire together by
   a. ruling as an absolute emperor.
   b. appointing Macedonians to run parts of the empire.
   c. governing with Persians, Greeks, and Macedonians.
   d. appointing a council of Athenian nobles.

_____ 9. Hellenistic culture was a blend of
   a. Greek, Mediterranean, and Asian cultures.
   b. the best Persian cultures.
   c. Greek and African culture.
   d. Athenian and Trojan culture.

_____ 10. After Alexander's death,
   a. Egypt conquered the empire.
   b. the empire grew.
   c. Greeks regained control of the empire.
   d. infighting tore apart the empire.

Name _____ Class _____ Date _____

CHAPTER 6

Daily Quiz 6.4

The Spread of Hellenistic Culture

TRUE/FALSE Mark each statement *T* if it is true or *F* if it is false. If false explain why.

_____ 1. During the Hellenistic Age, the gap between rich and poor increased.

_____ 2. Alexandria, a city in Egypt, gained power and prestige during the Hellenistic Age.

_____ 3. Hellenistic women became freer than before and gained some rights.

_____ 4. Despite Hellenistic influence, other cultures retained their identities.

_____ 5. Hellenistic culture made people lose interest in religion.

_____ 6. Philosophies such as Cynicism encouraged ruler worship.

_____ 7. Skeptics taught that all knowledge is uncertain in a changing universe.

_____ 8. Stoics believed that the aim of life is to seek pleasure.

_____ 9. Hellenistic doctors learned about the human body by using the Egyptian art of embalming.

_____ 10. Hellenistic scientists came to believe that the sun revolved around the planets.

Name _____ Class _____ Date _____

 Daily Quiz 7.1

Founding the Roman Republic

FILL IN THE BLANK *(10 points each)* For each of the following statements, fill in the blank with the appropriate word, phrase, or name.

1. Rome grew out of villages located along the _____ River.

2. The _____ brought a written language and engineering skills to the early Romans.

3. Rome eventually replaced its monarchy with a _____, where the people elected officials to run the state.

4. The Roman _____ was the most powerful part of the government.

5. The magistrates were made up of consuls, _____, and censors.

6. _____ helped to oversee the behavior of the Roman people.

7. Roman government used a system of _____ to keep a balance of power.

8. _____ were elected to make sure the actions of Roman lawmakers were fair.

9. _____ were commoners who fought to gain powers and rights.

10. The Twelve Tables were the _____.

Name _____ Class _____ Date _____

Daily Quiz 7.2

Rome Expands Its Borders

MULTIPLE CHOICE *(10 points each)* For each of the following, write the letter of the best choice in the space provided.

_____ 1. Rome made an enemy of a city in North Africa named
  a. Phoenicia.
  b. Sicily.
  c. Punic.
  d. Carthage.

_____ 2. Rome built a navy and attacked Carthage by sea during the
  a. First Carthage War.
  b. First Punic War.
  c. Rome-Carthage War.
  d. Roman Naval War.

_____ 3. "Boarding bridges" gave Romans a way to
  a. climb into forts.
  b. quickly board enemy ships.
  c. quickly cross rivers.
  d. quickly cross mountains.

_____ 4. Carthage again attacked Rome under the leadership of
  a. Scipio.
  b. Polybius.
  c. Hannibal.
  d. Zama.

_____ 5. In the Second Punic War, Carthage tried to defeat Rome by destroying
  a. ships with boarding bridges.
  b. trade routes to Rome.
  c. Rome's access to the Alps.
  d. the countryside and winning away Rome's allies.

_____ 6. Carthage was defeated again by a Roman general named
  a. Scipio.
  b. Cannae.
  c. Hannibal.
  d. Polybius.

_____ 7. Rome's victory in the Second Punic War gave it control of
  a. Phoenicia.
  b. Cannae.
  c. the western Mediterranean.
  d. North Africa.

_____ 8. The Third Punic War began because Rome decided to
  a. give protection to Greek cities.
  b. join Hannibal.
  c. attack Macedonia.
  d. destroy Carthage.

_____ 9. As a result of the Third Punic War, Rome
  a. gained control of the Mediterranean region.
  b. lost to Macedonia.
  c. and Carthage became allies.
  d. became Spain's ally.

_____ 10. After the Punic Wars, a class of wealthy Roman business people called _____ came to power
  a. Spartacus
  b. nobles
  c. equites
  d. Scipians

CHAPTER 7

Daily Quiz 7.3
The Birth of the Roman Empire

TRUE/FALSE Mark each statement *T* if it is true or *F* if it is false. If false explain why.

_____ 1. The Gracchi were murdered because they attempted social reform.

_____ 2. Roman allies who did not have full citizenship rebelled against the Senate and started the Gracchi Wars.

_____ 3. Private armies, like those raised by Marius and Sulla, helped strengthen the republic.

_____ 4. Julius Caesar gained control during the First Triumvirate by defeating Egypt.

_____ 5. Julius Caesar controlled Rome by reducing the power of the Senate.

_____ 6. After Julius Caesar's assassination, Brutus, Cassius, and Lepidus formed the Second Triumvirate.

_____ 7. An alliance between Antony and Cleopatra was defeated by Octavian.

_____ 8. Augustus Caesar's reign began a peaceful period called the Pax Romana.

_____ 9. One of the Pax Romana emperors, Claudius, destroyed Rome with a fire.

_____ 10. Marcus Aurelius was a warlike emperor who sought to expand Rome.

Name _____ Class _____ Date _____

 Daily Quiz 7.4

Roman Society and Culture

SHORT ANSWER *(10 points each)* Use the space provided to answer the following questions.

1. How did Rome keep such a large empire unified? _____

2. How did the code of the Twelve Tables change during the empire? _____

3. What was the most important occupation in the empire? _____

4. Why were good roads and bridges important to the Roman Empire? _____

5. What was the role of the army in the empire? _____

6. Did people in Rome have equal lives? _____

7. Who was the center of Roman family life? _____

8. What did Romans build to bring waters to the cities? _____

9. What did Virgil, Horace, and Ovid have in common? _____

10. What language did the Romans spread throughout their empire? _____

Name _____ Class _____ Date _____

CHAPTER 

Daily Quiz 7.5

The Rise of Christianity

MATCHING *(10 points each)* In the space provided, write the letter of the term or place that matches each description. Some answers will not be used.

_____ 1. Zealots

_____ 2. Messiah

_____ 3. Wailing Wall

_____ 4. rabbis

_____ 5. Jesus

_____ 6. resurrection and ascension

_____ 7. martyrs

_____ 8. Constantine

_____ 9. pope

_____ 10. council at Nicaea

a. banned Jews from Jerusalem

b. heads of Christian churches in each city

c. emphasized that people must love God above all else

d. belief that Jesus rose from the dead and then was taken to heaven

e. wanted to rebel against Rome to protect Judaism

f. scholars who interpreted scripture and led Jewish congregations

g. four books that make up the New Testament in the Bible

h. Roman emperor who supported Christianity

i. wrote down the main beliefs of the Christian church

j. Greek word for Messiah

k. western wall that survived the Roman attack on Jerusalem

l. people put to death for their beliefs

m. one who died for the sins of others

n. head of entire Christian church

Name _____ Class _____ Date _____

Daily Quiz 7.6

The Fall of the Western Empire

TRUE/FALSE Mark each statement *T* if it is true or *F* if it is false. If false explain why.

_____ 1. Roman emperors devalued silver coins to pay for the defense of the empire.

_____ 2. Diocletian saved the empire by ruling as an absolute monarch.

_____ 3. Constantine created a second capital in the East, Constantinople, to defend that region of the empire.

_____ 4. After Constantine's death, the western empire grew stronger than the eastern empire.

_____ 5. The Goths and the Vandals were invaders from the north who sacked Rome.

_____ 6. The Huns, led by Attila, successfully invaded Rome.

_____ 7. The tribes who invaded Rome kept its culture and continued Rome's development.

_____ 8. The Eastern Roman Empire declined soon after the Western Roman Empire.

_____ 9. Heavy taxes and defense and maintenance of the empire contributed to the decline of the empire.

_____ 10. The gap between Roman rich and poor created discontent and lack of loyalty to the empire.

Name _____ Class _____ Date _____

Daily Quiz 8.1
Africa's Early History

SHORT ANSWER *(10 points each)* Use the space provided to answer the following questions.

1. How did the geographical features of most African rivers both help and hurt Africa's development? _____

2. How has the climate of the Sahara changed? _____

3. What are savannas? _____

4. What are jungles? _____

5. How did the climate of the rain forests affect early African's health? _____

6. What are Bantu? _____

7. What are griots? _____

8. What do languages and musical instruments tell scholars about early Africa? _____

9. What role did women play in early African society? _____

10. Who had the most authority in African villages? _____

Name _____ Class _____ Date _____

Daily Quiz 8.2
The Kingdoms of Kush and Aksum

MULTIPLE CHOICE *(10 points each)* For each of the following, write the letter of the best choice in the space provided.

_____ 1. Because of its location, early Kush was influenced by
   a. Carthage.
   b. Egypt.
   c. Athens.
   d. Rome.

_____ 2. Kush showed it increased its power in 710 B.C. when it conquered
   a. Upper Egypt and ruled over a unified Egypt.
   b. Aksum and ruled over Egypt and Aksum.
   c. Carthage and ruled over North Africa.
   d. North Africa and ruled over the Mediterranean region.

_____ 3. Kush rebuilt itself and thrived after an invasion from
   a. Aksum.
   b. Nubia.
   c. Egypt.
   d. Assyria.

_____ 4. Kush trade benefited from the kingdom's location, which was near
   a. Aksum.
   b. the Red Sea and the Nile.
   c. the Indian Ocean.
   d. the rain forests.

_____ 5. Kush's decline may have been related to
   a. the loss of trading routes to rivals.
   b. infighting among Kush leadership.
   c. invasion from Egypt.
   d. invasion from Rome.

_____ 6. Aksum benefited from
   a. trade through Kush.
   b. trade through Egypt.
   c. conquering Egypt.
   d. joining forces with Carthage.

_____ 7. King 'Ēzānā increased Aksum's power when he conquered
   a. Meroë.
   b. Egypt.
   c. Kush.
   d. Assyria.

_____ 8. King 'Ēzānā's style of leadership was affected by his
   a. relationship with Kush.
   b. conversion to Judaism.
   c. relationship with Egypt.
   d. conversion to Christianity.

_____ 9. Aksum's trade eventually was affected by
   a. a lack of demand.
   b. competition from Kush.
   c. overuse of land and forests.
   d. drought.

_____ 10. Aksum's decline was related to
   a. a loss of trade routes to Persia.
   b. war with Persia.
   c. war with Kush.
   d. a lack of strong leadership.

Copyright © by Holt, Rinehart and Winston. All rights reserved.
World History: The Human Journey

Name _____ Class _____ Date _____

CHAPTER 8

Daily Quiz 8.3
Trading States of Africa

TRUE/FALSE Mark each statement *T* if it is true or *F* if it is false. If false explain why.

_____ 1. Sailing ships found that monsoon winds made trading on the East African coastline almost impossible.

_____ 2. Trade with Arab countries brought Islam to Africa.

_____ 3. Persian and Arabic influences helped develop the Bantu culture.

_____ 4. Kilwa was one of the great chiefs of the East African coastal city-states.

_____ 5. The Shona people gained control over the Zimbabwe gold trade.

_____ 6. Great Zimbabwe probably declined because of attacks from barbarian invaders.

_____ 7. Ghana was a West African kingdom that grew wealthy in the gold-for-salt exchange.

_____ 8. The Mali leader Mansa Mūsā built Timbuktu into a leading center of Islamic learning and culture.

_____ 9. Sonni 'Alī and Mohammed I Askia made the Songhai empire a great commercial center.

_____ 10. The Songhai Empire grew stronger after invading Morocco.

Name _____ Class _____ Date _____

Daily Quiz 9.1

The Earliest Americans

FILL IN THE BLANK *(10 points each)* For each of the following statements, fill in the blank with the appropriate word, phrase, or name.

1. North America's Rocky Mountains are called the _____ in South America.

2. The world's second longest river, the _____, flows through South America.

3. The Americas were separated from Asia by a narrow strip of water called a _____.

4. The Americas' earliest people probably migrated over land bridges from _____.

5. Early people probably migrated to America because of _____.

6. A common theme of Native American creation myths is _____.

7. Because of the large mammals in the Americas, the earliest people probably survived as _____.

8. People in the Americas turned to agriculture after _____.

9. Native American farmers did not invent plows because there were no _____.

10. The success of farming in the Americas encouraged people to _____.

Name _____ Class _____ Date _____

Daily Quiz 9.2
Cultures of North America

TRUE/FALSE Mark each statement *T* if it is true or *F* if it is false. If false explain why.

_____ 1. People on North America's northwestern coast survived mainly by hunting.

_____ 2. Totem poles represented a family's material wealth.

_____ 3. Potlatches were gatherings at which a clan's chief would give away the clan's possessions as a mark of social status.

_____ 4. The Hohokam people lived in the southwestern part of North America.

_____ 5. The Hohokam survived by fishing in the Gila River until it dried up.

_____ 6. The Pueblo lived in homes made of wood and grass.

_____ 7. The Great Plains people primarily lived by hunting buffalo.

_____ 8. Dogs were regarded as sacred in the Great Plains culture.

_____ 9. Hopewell and Mississippian cultures made their homes in large earthen mounds.

_____ 10. Evidence suggests that the Eastern Woodlands people traded with others across the country.

Name _____ Class _____ Date _____

Daily Quiz 9.3

Mesoamerica and Andean South America

SHORT ANSWER *(10 points each)* Use the space provided to answer the following questions.

1. What was the earliest known culture in Mexico? _____

2. Did the Maya have a writing system? What was it? _____

3. What did the Maya use astronomy for? _____

4. Who was Quetzalcoatl? _____

5. What became the most powerful civilization in Mexico? _____

6. What group dominated Aztec society? _____

7. How did the Aztec worship their sun god? _____

8. What caused the decline of the Aztec Empire? _____

9. What does the name *Inca* mean? _____

10. How did the Inca emperors try to unite the empire? _____

Name _____ Class _____ Date _____

CHAPTER

Modern Chapter 1

Daily Quiz 10.1

The Byzantine Empire

MULTIPLE CHOICE *(10 points each)* For each of the following, write the letter of the best choice in the space provided.

_____ 1. The Justinian Code was based on the idea that
  a. a strong military should dictate the law.
  b. people were judged according to social status.
  c. people should be ruled by laws, not by leaders' whims.
  d. people should be ruled as the emperor pleases.

_____ 2. Justinian's wife, Theodora, encouraged him to
  a. be tougher on peasants.
  b. invade Rome.
  c. increase peasants' rights.
  d. increase women's rights.

_____ 3. The Byzantine Empire increased after the military victories of
  a. Belisarius.
  b. Theodora.
  c. Justinian.
  d. Marcus Aurelius.

_____ 4. The Byzantine Empire helped create alliances with foreign powers through
  a. marriage.
  b. siege.
  c. taxation.
  d. guerrilla attacks.

_____ 5. The Byzantine navy used "Greek fire," which was
  a. an early type of fuel.
  b. burning spears.
  c. liquid that burst into flames.
  d. liquid to strengthen sails.

_____ 6. The location of Constantinople helped the Byzantines control
  a. the empire's wealth.
  b. tax policies.
  c. travel to Africa.
  d. trade between Asia and Europe.

_____ 7. The Iconoclastic Controversy was a battle about the
  a. Muslims and Christians.
  b. use of icons in the Christian church.
  c. taxation of church property.
  d. power of the pope.

_____ 8. To teach the Bible to Slavs, Cyril and Methodius created the
  a. Slavic alphabet.
  b. Method alphabet.
  c. Cyrillic alphabet.
  d. Eastern alphabet.

_____ 9. The Seljuq Turks' capture of Asia Minor affected the Byzantines because the area
  a. was full of gold.
  b. protected the empire.
  c. provided food and soldiers.
  d. provided animals for food and clothing.

_____ 10. The Byzantine Empire was finally conquered by
  a. the Ottoman Turks.
  b. the Seljuq Turks.
  c. western forces.
  d. the Balkans.

Copyright © by Holt, Rinehart and Winston. All rights reserved.

Name _____ Class _____ Date _____

Modern Chapter 1

Daily Quiz 10.2

The Rise of Russia

FILL IN THE BLANK *(10 points each)* For each of the following statements, fill in the blank with the appropriate word, phrase, or name.

1. The fertile, grassy plain south of eastern Europe and Central Asia is called the _____.

2. A network of _____ provide transportation throughout the plain between eastern Europe and Central Asia.

3. Eastern Europe was primarily populated by _____.

4. Vikings moved into Eastern Europe to build _____.

5. _____, the leader of the Rus, took control of the area around Kiev.

6. Kievan Russia was governed by princes and a council of nobles called _____.

7. Kievan princes could discuss important matters with the people at a town meeting, or _____.

8. Yaroslav the Wise introduced the Pravda Russkia, a _____.

9. _____ ordered Kievan Russia to become Christian.

10. Kievan Russia had two agricultural regions, the steppe and the _____.

Name _____ Class _____ Date _____

CHAPTER 10

Daily Quiz 10.3
Russia and the Mongols

Modern Chapter 1

TRUE/FALSE Mark each statement *T* if it is true or *F* if it is false. If false explain why.

_____ 1. Kievan Russia declined because of peasant uprisings.

_____ 2. During the 1200s, Polovtsy invaders conquered almost all of Kievan Russia.

_____ 3. Mongols maintained control of Kievan Russia through heavy taxation.

_____ 4. Slavic hostility toward western Europe increased when Poland converted to western Christianity.

_____ 5. Prince Ivan I gained power for Moscow by defeating Mongol leaders.

_____ 6. Ivan III became the first ruler of an independent Russia.

_____ 7. Ivan the Terrible made himself czar of Russia, and ruled under the advice of a council called the *oprichniki*.

_____ 8. During Ivan the Terrible's rule, Russia declined because of his harsh leadership.

_____ 9. The Orthodox Church in Russia gained power by acquiring land.

_____ 10. Moscow became the center of the "third Rome" after Constantinople returned to western Christianity.

Name _____ Class _____ Date _____

Modern Chapter **2**

Daily Quiz 11.1
The Rise of Islam

MATCHING *(10 points each)* In the space provided, write the letter of the term or place that matches each description. Some answers will not be used.

_____ 1. bedouins
_____ 2. Mecca
_____ 3. Muhammad
_____ 4. Kaaba
_____ 5. hijrah
_____ 6. Islam
_____ 7. Muslim
_____ 8. Qur'an
_____ 9. jihad
_____ 10. mosque

a. prophet who founded Islam
b. means "the struggle to defend the faith"
c. a building in Mecca that housed idols
d. title of respect given to the leader of a tribe
e. means "flight" or "migration"
f. follower of Islam
g. nomadic Arab herders
h. means "submission to the will of God"
i. powerful Arab trading center and first place of worship for Muhammad's followers
j. holy book of Islam
k. Muslim place of worship

Name _____ Class _____ Date _____

Modern Chapter 2

Daily Quiz 11.2
The Spread of Islam

MULTIPLE CHOICE *(10 points each)* For each of the following, write the letter of the best choice in the space provided.

_____ 1. After Muhammad's death, Abū Bakr was named "successor to the Prophet," or
   a. king.
   b. prophet.
   c. caliph.
   d. second prophet.

_____ 2. Islam expanded into Persia under the leadership of
   a. 'Umar.
   b. Abū Bakr.
   c. Iraq.
   d. Muhammad.

_____ 3. The Muslim community split over
   a. the worship of icons.
   b. how to appoint a caliph.
   c. the teachings of the Qur'an.
   d. treatment of Christians.

_____ 4. The Sunni believed that the Muslim people should
   a. settle their own religious matters.
   b. support the leaders' decisions.
   c. search for a new caliph.
   d. rewrite the Qur'an.

_____ 5. Those who supported the decisions of the imams were known as
   a. the Shi'ah.
   b. the 'Alī.
   c. the 'Uthmān.
   d. Mu'awiyah.

_____ 6. The Sufi Muslims believe in
   a. living a simple life.
   b. converting nonbelievers.
   c. expanding Islam.
   d. the Shi'ah.

_____ 7. Tāriq brought Islam to
   a. France.
   b. Syria.
   c. Spain.
   d. Rome.

_____ 8. The Moors were Muslims who lived in
   a. Spain.
   b. Constantinople.
   c. Gibraltar.
   d. France.

_____ 9. After the Moors, the next group to expand Muslim territory was the
   a. Syrians.
   b. Turks.
   c. Moors.
   d. Iraqis.

_____ 10. The Turks were ruled by a
   a. sultan.
   b. caliph.
   c. Sufi.
   d. Tariq.

Name _____ Class _____ Date _____

Modern Chapter **2**

Daily Quiz 11.3
Islamic Civilization

FILL IN THE BLANK *(10 points each)* For each of the following statements, fill in the blank with the appropriate word, phrase, or name.

1. The Islamic Empire became wealthy as a result of _____.

2. The Muslim Empire was governed by _____, who reported to caliphs in Baghdad, Cairo, and Córdoba.

3. Both religious life and daily life in the Islamic Empire were guided by the _____.

4. According to the Qur'an, Muslims were to free their _____.

5. The laws of the Qur'an said that women who _____ could keep their own money and remarry.

6. The Muslim world produced many great scientists and physicians, making Baghdad and _____ centers of medical learning.

7. One invention that the Muslims adapted and improved was the Greek _____, which could be used by sailors for navigation.

8. Muslim mathematician Al-Khwārizmī wrote about *al-jabr*, which became the basis of _____.

9. Islamic religious art relied on geometric and floral designs because Muslims were not allowed _____.

10. The Muslim story of _____ became the basis of *The Thousand and One Nights*.

Name _____ Class _____ Date _____

Modern Chapter 3

Daily Quiz 12.1

China under the Sui, Tang, and Sung Dynasties

TRUE/FALSE *(10 points each)* Mark each statement *T* if it is true or *F* if it is false. If false explain why.

_____ 1. The Sui dynasty was short-lived because of failed attempts at expansion.

_____ 2. The Tang dynasty further closed off China to other nations and cultures.

_____ 3. During the Tang dynasty, Xi'an became a large, international city.

_____ 4. Du Fu wrote poetry that celebrated military glory.

_____ 5. Hinduism became the primary religion in China during the time Empress Wu ruled.

_____ 6. Zen, a Buddhist sect, stressed meditation as a way to enlightenment.

_____ 7. The Tang dynasty encouraged the growth of the Buddhist monasteries.

_____ 8. Under the Sung dynasty, China defeated Mongol invaders.

_____ 9. High taxes forced many Tang dynasty peasants to sell their farms and become tenant farmers.

_____ 10. Footbinding became a sign of a man's economic success.

Name _____ Class _____ Date _____

Modern Chapter 3

Daily Quiz 12.2
The Mongol Empire

MULTIPLE CHOICE *(10 points each)* For each of the following, write the letter of the best choice in the space provided.

_____ 1. The Mongol army featured highly skilled
   a. weaponry experts.
   b. geography corps.
   c. diplomatic corps.
   d. platoons.

_____ 2. The Mongol Empire was greatly expanded under the "Universal Ruler,"
   a. Kublai Khan.
   b. Genghis Khan.
   c. Batu.
   d. Ivan the Terrible.

_____ 3. All of China and part of Southeast Asia were conquered by
   a. Kublai Khan.
   b. Genghis Khan.
   c. Batu.
   d. Marco Polo.

_____ 4. The Mongols invaded Europe and took control of Russia under the leadership of
   a. Kublai Khan.
   b. Genghis Khan.
   c. Batu.
   d. Khanbalik.

_____ 5. Europeans called the Mongols the "Golden Horde" because of
   a. the color of their armor.
   b. the color of their tents.
   c. their wealth.
   d. their generosity.

_____ 6. The Mongols aided China by
   a. limiting the population.
   b. offering tax relief.
   c. improving roads and communication.
   d. giving land to peasants.

_____ 7. There was a growing resentment toward Mongol rule because of
   a. harsh taxes.
   b. the Mongols' treatment of missionaries.
   c. military practices.
   d. religious differences.

_____ 8. Kublai Khan increased European contact with China by employing whom as his special representative?
   a. Batu
   b. Genghis Khan
   c. the pope
   d. Marco Polo

_____ 9. Under Mongol rule, the Chinese could not
   a. hold government office.
   b. own land.
   c. go to school.
   d. choose a religion.

_____ 10. Lasting influences of the Mongols in China included
   a. a weakened emperor.
   b. a more powerful emperor.
   c. a more isolated country.
   d. equality among classes.

Name _____ Class _____ Date _____

CHAPTER 12

Daily Quiz 12.3

Modern Chapter 3

Japan, Korea, and Southeast Asia

FILL IN THE BLANK *(10 points each)* For each of the following statements, fill in the blank with the appropriate word, phrase, or name.

1. Japan is made up of a string of thousands of _____.

2. An early Japanese religion, _____, is based on a belief in nature spirits.

3. The world's first novel, _____, written in Japanese, was evidence that Japanese culture was becoming more independent.

4. In the 1100s, Japanese emperors lost power to generals who held the title of _____.

5. During the feudal era, wealthy Japanese landowners protected themselves with warriors called _____.

6. _____ was not just a religion in Japan, but also a significant cultural influence.

7. The Korean Peninsula was dominated by the Chinese in the mid-1200s until the _____ overthrew the Mongols in 1392.

8. Korean government was heavily influenced by a small class of _____.

9. Vietnam showed the effects of Chinese culture in its adoption of _____ as a religion and a philosophy.

10. The Indian-influenced _____ Empire controlled most of Southeast Asia.

Daily Quiz 13.1

Modern Chapter **4**

The Rise of the Franks

MATCHING *(10 points each)* In the space provided, write the letter of the term or place that matches each description. Some answers will not be used.

_____ 1. medieval

_____ 2. Franks

_____ 3. Clovis

_____ 4. Carolingians

_____ 5. Charlemagne

_____ 6. Emperor of the Romans

_____ 7. *missi dominici*

_____ 8. Treaty of Verdun

_____ 9. Magyars

_____ 10. Vikings

a. dynasty of Frankish kings

b. title given to Charlemagne by pope

c. divided Charlemagne's empire among his sons

d. period between the classical age and beginnings of the modern world

e. officials who oversaw laws in Charlemagne's empire

f. united much of western Europe and stopped Moors advance across the Pyrenees

g. Charlemagne's son

h. Scandinavian explorers and invaders, known for their terrifying raids

i. Merovingian king who gained control of northern and southwestern Gaul

j. nomadic invaders, who settled in Hungary

k. helped the pope defeat the Lombards

l. Germanic people

Name _____ Class _____ Date _____

Modern Chapter 4

Daily Quiz 13.2

Feudalism and the Manorial System

MULTIPLE CHOICE *(10 points each)* For each of the following, write the letter of the best choice in the space provided.

_____ 1. Much of medieval Europe was run by a system known as feudalism, or rule by
  a. local clergy.
  b. local lords.
  c. elected landowners.
  d. a king.

_____ 2. A grant of land to be used, but not owned, by a noble was known as a
  a. fief.
  b. vassal.
  c. divot.
  d. square.

_____ 3. Anyone who received a grant of land from a powerful lord was known as a
  a. fief.
  b. landowner.
  c. serf.
  d. vassal.

_____ 4. Primogeniture is the system whereby land passes from a
  a. husband to a wife.
  b. man to a brother.
  c. father to his favorite son.
  d. father to his eldest son.

_____ 5. A woman who gave up her property to her husband could regain it if
  a. she sued for it.
  b. divorced her husband.
  c. her husband died.
  d. her son died.

_____ 6. During the Middle Ages, a vassal promised loyalty to his
  a. king.
  b. church.
  c. peasants.
  d. lord.

_____ 7. Decrees against violence and destruction near churches during war were issued by
  a. medieval kings.
  b. lords.
  c. the church.
  d. scholars.

_____ 8. A lord got most of his income from
  a. city taxes.
  b. the work of his peasants.
  c. the sale of herd animals.
  d. trade.

_____ 9. A man could gain additional land through
  a. marriage.
  b. successful farming.
  c. holding local office.
  d. paying additional taxes.

_____ 10. The code that guided knights' behavior was
  a. feudalism.
  b. the codes of war.
  c. the cheval principal.
  d. chivalry.

Name _____ Class _____ Date _____

CHAPTER 13

Daily Quiz 13.3

Modern Chapter **4**

The Church

TRUE/FALSE Mark each statement *T* if it is true or *F* if it is false. If false explain why.

_____ 1. Part of the medieval church's power was based in its ownership of vast amounts of land.

_____ 2. The church had little political power because of strong central governments in European countries.

_____ 3. Parish priests' high rank within the church was based on their ability to administer sacraments.

_____ 4. Kings usually appointed bishops based on their political or family ties.

_____ 5. The pope's most important advisors were the archbishops.

_____ 6. The strict monastic lifestyle was meant to show an extreme devotion to God.

_____ 7. The church could reward an entire region and its churches by issuing an interdict.

_____ 8. Anyone who questioned the church's principles or beliefs was called a heretic.

_____ 9. Poor people could receive money, or tithes, granted by the church.

_____ 10. Simony was the process by which bishops were elected.

Name _____ Class _____ Date _____

CHAPTER  Daily Quiz 13.4

Modern Chapter 4   **The Struggle for Power in England and France**

FILL IN THE BLANK *(10 points each)* For each of the following statements, fill in the blank with the appropriate word, phrase, or name.

1. The Anglo-Saxons divided the kingdoms of England into districts called _____.

2. Edward the Confessor left no heir, so a fight for the English throne broke out between _____ and Harold of Wessex.

3. William established a feudal system for England in which the _____ was the ultimate authority.

4. Henry II's belief that clergy should be tried in royal courts led to a bitter fight with _____, the Archbishop of Canterbury.

5. King John was forced to accept _____, which outlined rights for the ordinary English citizen and mandated that the king be held to the same laws as the people.

6. The practice of having councils of nobles meet with representatives of the middle class became known as _____.

7. During the reign of Edward I, royal court decisions were collected and used to make future decisions. This collection of decisions became known as _____.

8. After the Carolingian kings, France was dominated by a line of _____ kings.

9. Philip the Fair established the _____, a representative body that included commoners as well as nobles.

10. Despite the efforts of the Capetian kings, France remained feudal rather than _____.

Name _____ Class _____ Date _____

CHAPTER 13

Modern Chapter 4

Daily Quiz 13.5

The Clash Over Germany and Italy

SHORT ANSWER *(10 points each)* For each of the following statements, fill in the blank with the appropriate word, phrase, or name.

1. Why did the pope name Otto I "Emperor of the Romans?" _____

2. What areas did Otto I rule? _____

3. Which emperor had enough power to select popes? _____

4. Which pope believed that the Catholic Church was the supreme power on Earth? _____

5. What issue caused a divide between Pope Gregory VII and Henry the IV? _____

6. What happened at the meeting at Canossa? _____

7. Which agreement limited imperial power over the German church? _____

8. What did Frederick Barbarossa want to do? _____

9. What league formed to fight off Frederick I? _____

10. Which powerful pope freely used excommunication and interdiction to maintain control over Europe? _____

Name _____ Class _____ Date _____

Daily Quiz 14.1

Modern Chapter **5**

The Crusades

MULTIPLE CHOICE *(10 points each)* For each of the following, write the letter of the best choice in the space provided.

_____ 1. The Seljuq Turks gained control of Palestine, also known as
   a. Constantinople.
   b. the Roman Empire.
   c. the Holy Land.
   d. the Christian Land.

_____ 2. The Byzantines asked Pope Urban II to protect them from the
   a. Seljuq Turks.
   b. Moors.
   c. British.
   d. Mongols.

_____ 3. The Crusades marked an attempt to
   a. spread Christianity.
   b. regain the Holy Land.
   c. unite Italy and Germany.
   d. unite the Roman Empire.

_____ 4. The march to Palestine was difficult because of
   a. a lack of leadership.
   b. a lack of soldiers.
   c. poor weapons.
   d. the hot weather.

_____ 5. The Turks in Jerusalem were unprepared because
   a. they lacked weapons.
   b. they were taken by surprise.
   c. of infighting.
   d. they lacked enough soldiers.

_____ 6. The crusaders captured Jerusalem and
   a. exiled the Muslims.
   b. exiled the Jews.
   c. made peace with the people.
   d. killed the Muslims and Jews.

_____ 7. The Second Crusade resulted in the crusaders'
   a. capture of Damascus.
   b. capture of Palestine.
   c. defeat at Damascus.
   d. defeat at Jerusalem.

_____ 8. The Third Crusade was the result of the recapture of Jerusalem by
   a. Frederick Barbarossa.
   b. Seljuq Turks.
   c. the Byzantines.
   d. Saladin.

_____ 9. The disastrous march by young Christians to regain the Holy Land is known as the
   a. Young People's Crusade.
   b. Children's Crusade.
   c. Fourth Crusade.
   d. Last Crusade.

_____ 10. One positive result of the Crusades was the
   a. pope's power increased.
   b. emperor's power increased.
   c. cultural exchange of ideas.
   d. French rise to power.

Name _____ Class _____ Date _____

Modern Chapter 5

Daily Quiz 14.2
The Revival of Trade

TRUE/FALSE Mark each statement *T* if it is true or *F* if it is false. If false explain why.

_____ 1. The feudal system of the Middle Ages helped increase trade.

_____ 2. Italian city-states increased trade by using the Crusades as a way to import goods from Asia.

_____ 3. Viking traders helped bring Asian goods to southern Europe.

_____ 4. Flanders, France, and the Netherlands formed the Hanseatic League to manage trade in northwestern Europe.

_____ 5. The Crusades helped to create a demand for Asian goods.

_____ 6. Traders were allowed to sell their goods at churches as long as they paid a tax to the church.

_____ 7. Trade among countries resulted in the need for money changers who converted the value of one currency to another.

_____ 8. In the domestic system, products are made and sold in the same country.

_____ 9. Bills of exchange helped merchants deposit money at one location, then withdraw it at another.

_____ 10. In a market economy, land, labor, and money are controlled by the government.

Name _____ Class _____ Date _____

CHAPTER 14

Modern Chapter **5**

Daily Quiz 14.3

The Growth of Towns

FILL IN THE BLANK *(10 points each)* For each of the following statements, fill in the blank with the appropriate word, phrase, or name.

1. Charters guaranteed the _____ of townspeople who broke away from the manors.

2. _____, or freedom from ever having to work on the manor, was one of the medieval townspeople's rights.

3. _____ meant that townspeople could freely sell their goods in the town market.

4. _____ guaranteed trading rights to the town merchants, as well as looked after the well being of its members.

5. _____ set rules and standards for artisans.

6. Young people learned a craft, like shoemaking or weaving, by first serving as an _____.

7. An artisan could graduate from being a _____ to a master by completing a masterpiece.

8. The middle class preferred the rule of _____ because they provided more stability in government.

9. The _____ was carried by fleas on rats.

10. Workers, in short supply because of the plague, were able to demand _____.

Name _____ Class _____ Date _____

Daily Quiz 14.4

Modern Chapter 5 — Life and Culture in the Middle Ages

MATCHING *(10 points each)* In the space provided, write the letter of the term or place that matches each description.

_____ 1. vernacular languages

_____ 2. troubadours

_____ 3. miracle, morality, and mystery plays

_____ 4. Dante

_____ 5. Chaucer

_____ 6. university

_____ 7. scholasticism

_____ 8. Peter Abelard

_____ 9. Thomas Aquinas

_____ 10. Gothic

a. "association of people"

b. style of architecture known for its elaborate arches and spires

c. English writer whose work popularized Middle English

d. short dramas with religious or biblical themes

e. wrote a book called *Sic et Non* that raised questions about the teachings of the church

f. everyday speech

g. poet whose work helped spread Tuscan dialect

h. monk whose work summarized medieval Christian thought

i. traveling singers who wrote poems about love and chivalry

j. philosophical attempt to bring faith and reason together

Name _____ Class _____ Date _____

Modern Chapter 5

Daily Quiz 14.5

Wars and the Growth of Nations

MULTIPLE CHOICE *(10 points each)* For each of the following, write the letter of the best choice in the space provided.

_____ 1. The Hundred Years' War began because England's Edward III
   a. attacked Scotland.
   b. attacked Ireland.
   c. claimed the German throne.
   d. claimed the French throne.

_____ 2. During the Hundred Years' War, England gained an advantage through its use of
   a. longbows.
   b. cavalry.
   c. excess manpower.
   d. the phalanx.

_____ 3. The use of weaponry, such as gunpowder and cannons,
   a. made battles shorter.
   b. made battles longer.
   c. made knights less important.
   d. made cavalry less important.

_____ 4. At the end of the Hundred Years' War,
   a. England controlled France
   b. England lost France.
   c. France controlled England.
   d. France split in two.

_____ 5. By the end of the Hundred Years' War, Parliament had become
   a. more powerful.
   b. less powerful.
   c. part of France.
   d. three separate bodies.

_____ 6. The War of the Roses was fought over
   a. the trade of roses.
   b. trade routes in France.
   c. control of the English throne.
   d. control of Parliament.

_____ 7. Charles VII gained control of France after
   a. Joan of Arc fought for him.
   b. England backed him.
   c. the Burgundys died out.
   d. Henry V's defeat.

_____ 8. After the Hundred Years' War, French kings became
   a. more powerful.
   b. less powerful.
   c. part of the English family.
   d. emperors of Rome.

_____ 9. Spain lost power in industry and trade after Ferdinand and Isabella
   a. instituted higher taxes.
   b. drove out non-Christians.
   c. executed business leaders.
   d. closed Spain's borders.

_____ 10. The Habsburgs gained power through
   a. increasing trade routes.
   b. peacefulness.
   c. buying church land.
   d. political marriages.

Name _____ Class _____ Date _____

Modern Chapter 5

Daily Quiz 14.6

Challenges to Church Power

TRUE/FALSE Mark each statement *T* if it is true or *F* if it is false. If false explain why.

_____ 1. Strong monarchies believed that the church helped a country's trade and industry.

_____ 2. During the 1200s, people began to question the church's wealth and its corrupt practices.

_____ 3. In 1294, Pope Boniface VIII agreed that the clergy should pay taxes.

_____ 4. Philip IV took power from the church by appointing popes himself.

_____ 5. The Babylonian Captivity refers to the years when the church controlled the popes.

_____ 6. Disputes over the clergy's control of France is known as the Great Schism.

_____ 7. The Council of Constance ended the Great Schism and elected one true pope.

_____ 8. *Defender of the Faith* supported the pope's control of wordly rulers.

_____ 9. John Wycliffe argued that individuals should be allowed to interpret the Bible without interference from clergy.

_____ 10. Jan Hus questioned the church's authority, which resulted in his banishment.

Name _____ Class _____ Date _____

Daily Quiz 15.1

Modern Chapter 6

The Italian Renaissance

MATCHING (*10 points each*) In the space provided, write the letter of the term or place that matches each description. Some answers will not be used.

_____ 1. means rebirth

_____ 2. powerful Italian family and patrons of the arts

_____ 3. scholars who based their studies on classical Greek and Roman literature.

_____ 4. poet and teacher who believed in learning by studying classical writers

_____ 5. writer who argued that rulers should pursue only power and success

_____ 6. wrote *The Book of the Courtier,* a book of manners

_____ 7. technique that allows artists to show depth on a flat canvas

_____ 8. early realist painter

_____ 9. artist who used science to make paintings more realistic

_____ 10. artist known for the frescoes on the ceiling of the Sistine Chapel

a. renaissance
b. Niccolò Machiavelli
c. perspective
d. humanists
e. Baldassare Castiglione
f. Leonardo da Vinci
g. Giotto
h. Francesco Petrarch
i. Michelangelo
j. Medici
k. Isabella d'Este
l. Rafael

Name _____ Class _____ Date _____

Modern Chapter **6**

Daily Quiz 15.2

The Northern Renaissance

MULTIPLE CHOICE *(10 points each)* For each of the following, write the letter of the best choice in the space provided.

_____ 1. Italian Renaissance ideas traveled north primarily because of
   a. war.
   b. the Crusades.
   c. trade and wealth.
   d. missionaries.

_____ 2. Johannes Gutenberg influenced the spread of ideas by
   a. printing with movable type.
   b. copying Italian paintings.
   c. learning printing from China.
   d. lecturing at universities.

_____ 3. The printing press had an economic impact by
   a. putting scribes out of work.
   b. making Gutenberg rich.
   c. bringing printing to Asia.
   d. giving jobs to artists.

_____ 4. Erasmus used the techniques of the Italian humanists to study and criticize
   a. Greek and Roman writings.
   b. the Christian Church.
   c. Islamic beliefs.
   d. the work of Italian thinkers.

_____ 5. Thomas More wrote about a *utopia,* or
   a. corrupt religion.
   b. corrupt society.
   c. ideal religion.
   d. ideal society.

_____ 6. Renaissance drama differed from classical drama because it
   a. was about Christianity.
   b. emphasized human actions.
   c. added actors with masks.
   d. created tragic heroes.

_____ 7. William Shakespeare's greatest talent was that he
   a. wrote like Marlowe.
   b. dramatized known stories.
   c. wrote lengthy prose.
   d. wrote epic poems.

_____ 8. The van Eyck brothers' art is notable for its
   a. realistic depictions of humans.
   b. symbolic representations.
   c. use of rich color.
   d. use of oil paints.

_____ 9. Brueghel's paintings show
   a. realistic religious scenes.
   b. symbolic religious scenes.
   c. ideal societies.
   d. everyday village life.

_____ 10. Northern art differed from Italian art because it
   a. used cooler colors.
   b. used oil paints.
   c. showed more realistic humans.
   d. showed ideal humans.

Name _____ Class _____ Date _____

CHAPTER 15

Modern Chapter 6

Daily Quiz 15.3

The Protestant Reformation

TRUE/FALSE Mark each statement *T* if it is true or *F* if it is false. If false explain why.

_____ 1. The fact that Germany was made up of independent states made it easier for rulers to control the national religion.

_____ 2. Martin Luther developed the belief that an inner faith in God, rather than actions and ceremonies, led to salvation.

_____ 3. Martin Luther's 95 theses protested the pope's control of German rulers.

_____ 4. Lutheran ministers were important because they interpreted the Bible for the people.

_____ 5. The Peace of Augsburg stated that the Holy Roman Emperor could dictate the religion of the German states.

_____ 6. The Anglican Church developed after English ministers printed an English language Bible.

_____ 7. *The Institutes of the Christian Religion* expressed the beliefs of John Calvin.

_____ 8. Calvinists believed in predestination, the idea that God decided at the beginning of time who would be saved.

_____ 9. A theocracy is a government that is ruled by religious leaders.

_____ 10. The Edict of Nantes gave Huguenots freedom of worship.

Name _____ Class _____ Date _____

Daily Quiz 15.4

Modern Chapter 6

The Catholic Reformation

FILL IN THE BLANK *(10 points each)* For each of the following statements, fill in the blank with the appropriate word, phrase, or name.

1. The _____ aimed to return the church to spiritual matters and stop the spread of Protestantism.

2. Pope Paul III brought the _____ to Rome to punish heretics and keep Catholics in the church.

3. In 1559, Pope Paul IV introduced the _____ to prevent Catholics from reading books that promoted Protestantism.

4. The _____ attempted to define Catholic doctrine.

5. In most cases, the Council of Trent reaffirmed the _____ beliefs that the Protestants had rejected.

6. The _____ were a religious order that took vows of poverty, chastity, and obedience to the pope.

7. One of the ways the Jesuits helped slow the spread of Protestantism was through an emphasis on _____.

8. The Jesuits combined Catholic doctrine and _____.

9. Both Catholics and Protestants showed little tolerance for _____.

10. The Protestants' break from the church led to an _____ in the power of government.

Name _____ Class _____ Date _____

CHAPTER

Modern Chapter **6**

Daily Quiz 15.5

Culture and Daily Life

MULTIPLE CHOICE *(10 points each)* For each of the following, write the letter of the best choice in the space provided.

_____ 1. Superstitions were a way for people of the Renaissance to
   a. explain God.
   b. explain politics.
   c. explain misfortune.
   d. entertain themselves.

_____ 2. For help, luck, or healing, villagers often turned to
   a. demons.
   b. wise folk.
   c. spirits.
   d. nuns.

_____ 3. Bad luck or misfortune might be blamed on
   a. a lack of faith.
   b. the wise folk.
   c. accidents.
   d. spirits.

_____ 4. Hysteria about witchcraft led to
   a. witch-hunts and executions.
   b. banishment.
   c. fines.
   d. increased church attendance.

_____ 5. The closeness of farming communities meant that individualism was
   a. not easily tolerated.
   b. encouraged.
   c. a matter for curiosity.
   d. typical in most villages.

_____ 6. The printing press popularized single printed sheets containing news or royal decrees that were called
   a. almanacs.
   b. pamphlets.
   c. newspapers.
   d. broadsides.

_____ 7. A popular book during the 1500s was the
   a. dictionary.
   b. almanac.
   c. encyclopedia.
   d. thesaurus.

_____ 8. Education became available to villages mostly because
   a. public schools were required.
   b. church leaders sponsored schools.
   c. parents started schools.
   d. universities started classes.

_____ 9. The standard of living increased because
   a. peasants had more income.
   b. lords became more generous.
   c. the church gave money to the poor.
   d. there were more people.

_____ 10. The rise of the city led to
   a. an increase in folklore.
   b. more belief in magic.
   c. less belief in magic.
   d. new superstitions.

Copyright © by Holt, Rinehart and Winston. All rights reserved.

World History: The Human Journey   Daily Quizzes

Name _____ Class _____ Date _____

Modern Chapter 7

Daily Quiz 16.1
The Scientific Revolution

TRUE/FALSE Mark each statement *T* if it is true or *F* if it is false. If false explain why.

_____ 1. Natural philosophers believed that a study of nature could explain science.

_____ 2. During the Renaissance, scientists developed the scientific method, which involves forming conclusions based on experimentation, repetition, and observation.

_____ 3. Copernicus introduced the idea that Earth was part of a geocentric universe.

_____ 4. Kepler devised the laws of planetary motion to prove Copernicus wrong.

_____ 5. Galileo Galilei's explanations of the universe and observations of motion confirmed Aristotle's beliefs about science.

_____ 6. Isaac Newton's laws of motion were at odds with the idea that God dictated every movement of humans and objects.

_____ 7. Both William Harvey and Andreas Vesalius made contributions to astronomy.

_____ 8. René Descartes argued that all assumptions had to be proven on the basis of known facts.

_____ 9. Francis Bacon believed truth could be discovered through reasoning and logic.

_____ 10. The Scientific Revolution was possible in part because of the printing press.

CHAPTER 16

Daily Quiz 16.2

Modern Chapter 7   **The Foundations of European Exploration**

FILL IN THE BLANK *(10 points each)* For each of the following statements, fill in the blank with the appropriate word, phrase, or name.

1. Europeans believed that the best way to improve trade was to find _____ to the East.

2. Navigation became easier and more reliable because of the invention of the _____.

3. The need to solidify business practices led to the _____.

4. Italian cities were among the first to produce coins with _____.

5. In a _____ company, investors who bought shares in the company became co-owners.

6. The world's increased wealth led to the theory of _____, which stated that a government should do all it could to increase its country's wealth.

7. Favorable balance of trade meant that a country _____.

8. A country could try to maintain a favorable balance of trade by putting a _____, or tax, on import goods.

9. Governments could encourage exports by giving out _____ to help residents start businesses.

10. Colonies offered people a chance to escape crowds, poverty, and _____.

Name _____ Class _____ Date _____

CHAPTER 16

Modern Chapter 7

Daily Quiz 16.3

Voyages of Portugal and Spain

MATCHING *(10 points each)* In the space provided, write the letter of the term or place that matches each description. Some answers will not be used.

_____ 1. "The Navigator"

_____ 2. found route to Indian Ocean in 1488

_____ 3. established trade routes from Europe to India in 1498

_____ 4. named discovery "West Indies" because he believed he had landed in Asia

_____ 5. time when goods began to travel between Europe and the Americas

_____ 6. line dividing new lands between Spain and Portugal

_____ 7. argued that new lands to the west were not part of Asia

_____ 8. found route to the Pacific Ocean

_____ 9. system that supported slave trade

_____ 10. slave voyage from Africa to the Americas

a. Christopher Columbus
b. Bartolomeu Dias
c. Amerigo Vespucci
d. Columbian Exchange
e. triangular trade
f. East Indies
g. Prince Henry
h. Treaty of Tordesillas
i. Ferdinand Magellan
j. Queen Isabella
k. Vasco da Gama
l. Middle Passage

Name _____ Class _____ Date _____

CHAPTER  16   Daily Quiz 16.4

Modern Chapter 7   **The Spanish and Dutch Empires**

MULTIPLE CHOICE *(10 points each)* For each of the following, write the letter of the best choice in the space provided.

_____ 1. Ponce de León extended Spanish exploration by landing on what is now
  a. Puerto Rico.
  b. Florida.
  c. Bermuda.
  d. California.

_____ 2. Spain invaded Mexico under the leadership of
  a. Ponce de León.
  b. Pánfilo de Narváez.
  c. Moctezuma II.
  d. Hernán Cortés.

_____ 3. One of Spain's most effective weapons during its attacks in Mexico was its
  a. Christianity.
  b. diplomacy.
  c. trade deals.
  d. horses.

_____ 4. The Spanish drive into South America was led by
  a. Francisco Pizarro.
  b. Hernán Cortés.
  c. Vasco da Gama.
  d. Ponce de León.

_____ 5. Spain primarily benefited from the Americas'
  a. gold mines.
  b. silver mines.
  c. cultural ideas.
  d. spice trade.

_____ 6. Conflicting interests between Spain and the Holy Roman Empire led Charles V to
  a. give Spain to Ferdinand I.
  b. give Spain to Philip II.
  c. give America to Ferdinand I.
  d. give the empire to Philip II.

_____ 7. Philip II treated the Dutch harshly because many were
  a. Calvinists.
  b. Lutherans.
  c. Catholics.
  d. Anglicans.

_____ 8. The Dutch gained control of European trade because of their
  a. sailing abilities.
  b. diplomatic skills.
  c. religious beliefs.
  d. silver mines.

_____ 9. The Dutch Empire succeeded in part because it colonized as traders, not as
  a. bankers.
  b. missionaries.
  c. explorers.
  d. Europeans.

_____ 10. The Spanish Empire declined because of all of the following except
  a. inflation from excess gold.
  b. lack of a middle class.
  c. religious divides.
  d. expulsion of the Jews and Moriscos.

Name _____ Class _____ Date _____

Modern Chapter **8**

Daily Quiz 17.1

The Ming and Qing Dynasties

FILL IN THE BLANK *(10 points each)* For each of the following statements, fill in the blank with the appropriate word, phrase, or name.

1. The Chinese were expert sailors who used the compass and large ships called _____.

2. Ming emperors did not pursue further exploration because they wanted China to be _____.

3. Worried about invasions, Ming emperors considered _____ more important than exploration.

4. The Ming dynasty divided society into four parts, from _____ at the top to merchants at the bottom.

5. The Qing dynasty had its roots in _____.

6. The Qing ordered all Chinese men to wear their hair in _____ to show submission to the Manchu.

7. The increase of city dwellers meant that _____ became more important, although the Chinese still regarded them as the lowest class.

8. Scholarship during the Qing dynasty included the development of _____, or the study of languages.

9. A rapidly growing population and government _____ weakened the Qing's rule.

10. Peasant discontent led to the _____.

Name _____ Class _____ Date _____

CHAPTER 17

Daily Quiz 17.2

Modern Chapter **8**

China and Europeans

MULTIPLE CHOICE *(10 points each)* For each of the following, write the letter of the best choice in the space provided.

_____ 1. To gain access to the Chinese emperor, the Jesuit missionaries used their knowledge of
  a. classical literature.
  b. philosophy.
  c. astronomy.
  d. Christianity.

_____ 2. The Chinese became suspicious of Christians because of their allegiance to
  a. the Holy Roman Emperor.
  b. Ignatius de Loyola.
  c. the pope.
  d. Jesus.

_____ 3. The British East India Company agreed to Chinese restrictions to gain a monopoly on
  a. tea.
  b. porcelain.
  c. cotton.
  d. sweet potatoes.

_____ 4. The belief that government should not be involved with trade is called
  a. mercantilism.
  b. free trade.
  c. open trade.
  d. monopolies.

_____ 5. The British began to trade opium for
  a. silk.
  b. coal.
  c. tobacco.
  d. tea.

_____ 6. The Chinese wanted to stop the opium trade because of its devastating effect on China's
  a. tea supply.
  b. silver supply.
  c. silk supply.
  d. cotton supply.

_____ 7. The British defeat of China in the Opium War resulted in the
  a. Treaty of Nanjing.
  b. Opium Treaty.
  c. China Treaty.
  d. Guangzhou Treaty.

_____ 8. Following the laws of a home country instead of the laws of the country in which a foreigner lives is called
  a. the Nanjing Rules.
  b. the Hong Kong Rules.
  c. extrasubjectivity.
  d. extraterritoriality.

_____ 9. As other countries arrived, the Chinese were forced to sign treaties under fear of invasion. These treaties were called
  a. "beneficial" treaties.
  b. "anti-beneficial" treaties.
  c. "unequal" treaties.
  d. "unfair" treaties.

_____ 10. The Taiping Rebellion was inspired in part by
  a. Buddhist teachings.
  b. Descartes' teachings.
  c. Jesuit teachings.
  d. Christian teachings.

Copyright © by Holt, Rinehart and Winston. All rights reserved.

Daily Quiz 17.3

Modern Chapter 8 The Tokugawa Shoguns in Japan

TRUE/FALSE Mark each statement *T* if it is true or *F* if it is false. If false explain why.

_____ 1. Oda Nobunaga was the most successful of the Ashikaga shogunate.

_____ 2. Hideyoshi defeated China to gain control of Korea.

_____ 3. As shogun, Tokugawa Ieyasu headed an absolute monarchy.

_____ 4. The Tokugawa shogunate kept the daimyo under control by forcing them to live in Edo while their families were hostages at home.

_____ 5. All samurai began using muskets brought to Japan by the Portuguese.

_____ 6. Fearing Christian influence, the shoguns forced the Portuguese out of Japan.

_____ 7. In the Tokugawa shogunate, scholars were the most important social class.

_____ 8. Commodore Matthew Perry, using heavily armed U.S. warships, forced the shogun to sign the Treaty of Kanagawa.

_____ 9. The U.S. obtained a monopoly on Japanese trade.

_____ 10. The shogunate was considered weak for signing treaties with foreigners.

Name _____ Class _____ Date _____

Modern Chapter **9**

Daily Quiz 18.1

The Ottoman Empire

MATCHING *(10 points each)* In the space provided, write the letter of the term or place that matches each description. Some answers will not be used.

_____ 1. ghazis
_____ 2. Osman
_____ 3. Janissaries
_____ 4. Timur
_____ 5. Murad II
_____ 6. Mehmed II
_____ 7. Süleyman
_____ 8. grand viziers
_____ 9. reaya
_____ 10. millets

a. elite Ottoman slave army
b. Turko-Mongol leader who defeated the Ottomans
c. powerful sultan who expanded the Ottoman Empire as far west as Vienna
d. defeated last European crusaders
e. leader of the Ottoman tribe
f. second in command to the sultans
g. "protected flock," or ordinary subjects
h. warriors for Islam
i. independent communities based on religious preferences
j. conquered Constantinople and made it capital of Ottoman Empire
k. formerly called Asia Minor

Name _____ Class _____ Date _____

Modern Chapter **9**

Daily Quiz 18.2
The Safavid Empire

MULTIPLE CHOICE *(10 points each)* For each of the following, write the letter of the best choice in the space provided.

_____ 1. The Safavid Empire was what is now mostly present-day
   a. Persia.
   b. Iran.
   c. Iraq.
   d. India.

_____ 2. The Safavids were descended from
   a. Osman.
   b. Timur.
   c. Safī od-Dīn.
   d. Safavid.

_____ 3. The Safavids were persecuted by Sunni Muslims because they were
   a. Islamic.
   b. Hindu.
   c. Theravada Buddhists.
   d. Shi'ah.

_____ 4. The Safavid army was known as the
   a. kizilbash.
   b. Red Army.
   c. Safavidi.
   d. Shi'ah.

_____ 5. The Safavid who brought together the land that would be the empire was
   a. Esmā'īl.
   b. Safī od-Dīn.
   c. Sunni.
   d. Safavid.

_____ 6. The title *shah* means
   a. "emperor."
   b. "sultan."
   c. "king of Persia."
   d. "king of kings."

_____ 7. The Safavids' Shi'ah beliefs caused them to be attacked by the Ottomans and
   a. Uzbeks.
   b. Mongols.
   c. Turks.
   d. Tajikis.

_____ 8. Shah 'Abbās regained Safavid territory by
   a. monopolizing trade routes.
   b. building a slave-soldier army.
   c. opening Safavid ports.
   d. converting to Sunni.

_____ 9. Shah 'Abbās built a carefully planned, beautiful capital called
   a. Istanbul.
   b. Eşfahān.
   c. Tahmāsp.
   d. Tehran.

_____ 10. The Safavids became known for their
   a. army.
   b. rice.
   c. carpets.
   d. horses.

Name _____ Class _____ Date _____

Daily Quiz 18.3

Modern Chapter 9

The Mughal Empire in India

FILL IN THE BLANK *(10 points each)* For each of the following statements, fill in the blank with the appropriate word, phrase, or name.

1. As Turkish Muslim rule in India weakened, Indian warrior princes, or _____, began to challenge them.

2. _____, a Mongol leader, conquered the Sultanate of Delhi and established the Mughal Empire.

3. Akbar won the support of his people by instituting an improved, more equitable _____ system.

4. Akbar encouraged literature written in Hindi and _____.

5. During Akbar's reign, other religions were _____.

6. Later in his reign, Akbar began to consider himself a _____, and established his own creed.

7. Shah Jahan is famous for buildings, such as the Taj Mahal and the _____, constructed during his reign.

8. Shah Jahan spent excessive amounts of money on buildings as a way of showing the world his _____.

9. Aurangzeb's rule reflected his strict _____ beliefs.

10. Aurangzeb's persecution of other _____ led to widespread rioting and rebellion.

Name _____ Class _____ Date _____

Modern Chapter 10

Daily Quiz 19.1
France in the Age of Absolutism

MULTIPLE CHOICE *(10 points each)* For each of the following, write the letter of the best choice in the space provided.

_____ 1. To unite France, Henry IV became a
 a. Lutheran.
 b. Catholic.
 c. Calvinist.
 d. Puritan.

_____ 2. As Louis XIII's advisor, Cardinal Richelieu strengthened the monarchy by
 a. lessening the nobles' power.
 b. lessening the pope's power.
 c. reforming taxes.
 d. encouraging trade.

_____ 3. The intendants' role in the provinces gave power back to the
 a. nobles.
 b. Catholics.
 c. military leaders.
 d. king.

_____ 4. France benefited from the Thirty Years' War because it
 a. weakened the Huguenots.
 b. weakened German princes.
 c. weakened the Holy Roman Empire.
 d. strengthened Germany.

_____ 5. Louis XIV's palace, Versailles, represented the grandeur of the monarchy, but also
 a. drained the French economy.
 b. offended the Catholic clergy.
 c. was an easy target.
 d. provided jobs.

_____ 6. Louis XIV believed in the divine right of kings, or
 a. that God made him king.
 b. that kings were gods.
 c. that kings were the best rulers.
 d. the right to conquer.

_____ 7. France became an economic power under the guide of
 a. Cardinal Richelieu.
 b. Jean-Baptiste Colbert.
 c. the Holy Roman Empire.
 d. the Duke of Sully.

_____ 8. Fearing France's strength and aggression, other European nations united to help create a
 a. balance of power.
 b. free market.
 c. European Union.
 d. stable currency.

_____ 9. European nations feared the impact of Louis XIV's grandson's inheritance of the Spanish throne, leading to the
 a. War of the Spanish Succession.
 b. French War of Succession.
 c. Fronde rebellions.
 d. Thirty Years' War.

_____ 10. The Treaty of Utrecht ruled that France and Spain could not be united, and gave French North American colonies to
 a. Spain.
 b. Britain.
 c. the Netherlands.
 d. Sweden.

Name _____ Class _____ Date _____

CHAPTER 19

Modern Chapter 10

Daily Quiz 19.2

Russia in the Age of Absolutism

TRUE/FALSE Mark each statement *T* if it is true or *F* if it is false. If false explain why.

_____ 1. Russia was both physically and culturally isolated from western Europe.

_____ 2. Peter the Great learned about the West by sending close advisors to study Western monarchies.

_____ 3. Peter the Great moved the capital of Russia to St. Petersburg to be closer to the Eastern Orthodox Church.

_____ 4. Peter the Great ordered changes in Russian dress and customs to further emulate the West.

_____ 5. The policy of "service nobility" meant that nobles were given political office based on rank.

_____ 6. Under Peter the Great's rule, nobles obtained more power.

_____ 7. Catherine the Great supported the arts as a way of educating the serfs.

_____ 8. Catherine's attempts to expand to the Black Sea met with defeat by the Turks.

_____ 9. Poland's weak government allowed Prussia, Austria, and Russia to seize for themselves territories in Poland.

_____ 10. During Catherine's reign, the divide between the rich and poor widened.

Name _____ Class _____ Date _____

Daily Quiz 19.3

Modern Chapter **10**   **Central Europe in the Age of Absolutism**

FILL IN THE BLANK *(10 points each)* For each of the following statements, fill in the blank with the appropriate word, phrase, or name.

1. The _____ allowed Maria Theresa to inherit Habsburg lands, but she could not become empress until her husband became emperor.

2. The Habsburg Empire's main rival was _____.

3. Frederick William, known as the _____, ruled Brandenburg-Prussia at the end of the Thirty Years' War.

4. Frederick I gathered all the lands in northern Germany under his rule, and took the title of _____.

5. Frederick I tried to emulate the court of _____ by keeping a large, extravagant court.

6. Frederick William I concentrated on creating a powerful _____.

7. The War of the Austrian Succession was the result of the _____ invasion of Silesia.

8. The Diplomatic Revolution saw Great Britain switch its allegiance from _____ to Prussia.

9. The Seven Years' War actually began in _____, where it was called the French and Indian War.

10. The Seven Years' War ended when European countries began to _____.

Name _____ Class _____ Date _____

Modern Chapter 10

Daily Quiz 19.4

The English Monarchy

MATCHING *(10 points each)* In the space provided, write the letter of the term or place that matches each description. Some answers will not be used.

_____ 1. first Tudor king

_____ 2. established the Anglican Church

_____ 3. tried to return England to Catholicism

_____ 4. long rule saw England maintain its power and flourish

_____ 5. plotted Elizabeth's assassination to return England to Catholicism

_____ 6. fleet that tried and failed to invade England

_____ 7. sect that believed the Anglican Church needed to be simplified

_____ 8. landowners, could serve in the House of Commons

_____ 9. merchants and professionals, able to serve in the House of Commons

_____ 10. ruler from the Stuart family who had an uneasy relationship with Parliament

a. Spanish Armada
b. Elizabeth I
c. Mary I
d. Mary Queen of Scots
e. Henry VIII
f. Phillip II
g. Henry VII
h. Puritans
i. James I
j. gentry
k. Edward VI
l. burgesses

Name _____ Class _____ Date _____

Daily Quiz 20.1

Modern Chapter 11

Civil War and Revolution

FILL IN THE BLANK *(10 points each)* For each of the following statements, fill in the blank with the appropriate word, phrase, or name.

1. Parliament had Charles I sign the _____, which limited the powers of the king.

2. Protests over Charles I's imposition of taxes led him to _____.

3. Realizing he needed new taxes to raise money, Charles I called what is known as the _____.

4. Disputes over how to manage an Irish rebellion started a _____.

5. Supporters of the king were known as Cavaliers, while the supporters of Parliament were called _____.

6. _____ led the Puritans' New Model Army against Charles I.

7. The Rump Parliament declared England a _____ and had Charles I executed.

8. As lord protector, Oliver Cromwell ruled as almost a _____, because of the power of his army.

9. The Instrument of Government of 1653 was an early form of a _____.

10. War with the Dutch erupted over England's passage of the _____.

Daily Quiz 20.2

Constitutional Monarchy in England

MATCHING *(10 points each)* In the space provided, write the letter of the term or place that matches each description. Some answers will not be used.

_____ 1. political party that supported hereditary right to rule

_____ 2. political party that supported Protestant rule and a strong Parliament

_____ 3. Catholic English king who believed in absolute rule

_____ 4. Protestant monarchs who succeeded James II

_____ 5. bloodless transfer of the monarchy

_____ 6. believed that people exchanged individual liberty for social order and safety

_____ 7. believed that people had certain rights with which a ruler cannot interfere

_____ 8. document that limited monarch's power and extended Parliament's power

_____ 9. granted some freedom to nonmembers of Anglican Church

_____ 10. where monarchy is head of state, but Parliament is primary governing body

a. Whig
b. Thomas Hobbes
c. Tory
d. the Glorious Revolution
e. habeas corpus
f. James II
g. Toleration Act
h. John Locke
i. English Bill of Rights
j. Mary II and William III
k. limited constitutional monarchy
l. the Restoration

Name _____ Class _____ Date _____

Daily Quiz 20.3

Modern Chapter 11

English Colonial Expansion

MULTIPLE CHOICE *(10 points each)* For each of the following, write the letter of the best choice in the space provided.

_____ 1. England's first claim in North America came from the voyages of
 a. John Cabot.
 b. Prince Henry.
 c. Christopher Columbus.
 d. the Dutch.

_____ 2. Sea dogs were
 a. dogs working on navy ships.
 b. low-ranking naval officers.
 c. foreign navies.
 d. traders and pirates.

_____ 3. Sir Francis Drake was the first English sea captain to
 a. sail around the world.
 b. sail across the Atlantic.
 c. land in South America.
 d. land in India.

_____ 4. The English used sea raids to disrupt colonization in North America by the
 a. Spanish.
 b. Dutch.
 c. French.
 d. Prussians.

_____ 5. The British East India Company extended British influence in India by establishing
 a. the wool trade.
 b. the slave trade.
 c. army posts.
 d. trading posts.

_____ 6. The Northwest Passage was a water route to Asia through
 a. South America.
 b. North America.
 c. Alaska.
 d. Russia.

_____ 7. Henry Hudson explored North American waterways for both the English and the
 a. Spanish.
 b. French.
 c. Dutch.
 d. Portuguese.

_____ 8. Founders of the early British colonies in North America hoped to
 a. make money.
 b. discover more land.
 c. promote Protestantism.
 d. escape punishment.

_____ 9. The British colony Barbados was a financial success because it
 a. offered religious freedom.
 b. was beautiful.
 c. was a central trading post.
 d. was worked by slaves.

_____ 10. British mercantilist policy forced colonies to
 a. only export to Britain.
 b. remain Anglican.
 c. vote Tory.
 d. enlist in the army.

Name _____ Class _____ Date _____

Daily Quiz 20.4

Modern Chapter 11

The Enlightenment

TRUE/FALSE Mark each statement *T* if it is true or *F* if it is false. If false explain why.

_____ 1. The 17th century is known as the Age of Enlightenment.

_____ 2. Rationalists believe that truth can be found simply by logical thought.

_____ 3. Natural law means that objects in nature act in predictable ways.

_____ 4. *The Encyclopedia*, by Diderot and d'Alembert, was a history of France.

_____ 5. In *The Spirit of Laws,* Baron de Montesquieu argued that an absolute monarchy was the ideal government.

_____ 6. Voltaire was twice imprisoned for his criticism of the French ruling class.

_____ 7. Jean-Jacques Rousseau stated that people are naturally corrupt and need a strong government to keep order.

_____ 8. Popular sovereignty is when a monarch is well liked.

_____ 9. Enlightened despotism is rule by a group of rationalist philosophes.

_____ 10. Mary Wollstonecraft wrote that women deserved the same rights as men.

Daily Quiz 20.5

The American Revolution

Modern Chapter 11

FILL IN THE BLANK *(10 points each)* For each of the following statements, fill in the blank with the appropriate word, phrase, or name.

1. Colonists opposed the _____, which placed a tax on many everyday documents.

2. Colonists who wanted to separate from Britain were called Patriots, and those who opposed independence were _____.

3. After the American Revolution began, colonial delegates met in Philadelphia in the _____.

4. The Declaration of Independence stated that all powers of government should come from the _____.

5. During the Revolutionary War, the British were disadvantaged by having to _____.

6. The American colonists knew the territory well, but their government suffered from a lack of _____.

7. When the war ended, the Americans sent _____ to negotiate a treaty.

8. The Articles of Confederation set up a government that gave the _____ the balance of power.

9. A _____ of government gave power to both a strong central government and states.

10. The Bill of Rights was added to the Constitution to give rights to _____.

Name _____ Class _____ Date _____

Daily Quiz 21.1

Modern Chapter 12

The Roots of Revolution

TRUE/FALSE Mark each statement *T* if it is true or *F* if it is false. If false explain why.

_____ 1. The Old Regime refers to time in France prior to 1789.

_____ 2. The First Estate referred to the French nobility.

_____ 3. The Third Estate, or bourgeoisie, consisted of civil servants and artisans.

_____ 4. French peasants had no way of influencing the laws of the land.

_____ 5. Worsening economic conditions angered French peasants, but the bourgeoisie were happy.

_____ 6. The French were suspicious of Marie-Antoinette's Prussian connection.

_____ 7. The French economy was weakened by Louis XV's constant need to finance wars.

_____ 8. The Estates General traditionally gave one vote to each estate.

_____ 9. The Third Estate demanded that a Fourth Estate be added to give a voice to the peasants.

_____ 10. The Third Estate locked out the other two estates and vowed to write a constitution.

Name _____ Class _____ Date _____

Modern Chapter 12

Daily Quiz 21.2

The French Revolution

MULTIPLE CHOICE *(10 points each)* For each of the following, write the letter of the best choice in the space provided.

_____ 1. When Louis XVI sent troops into Paris and Versailles, the people
 a. stormed Versailles.
 b. stormed the Bastille.
 c. stormed the Estates General.
 d. left Paris.

_____ 2. Rumors that the nobles were going to attack led to rioting called
 a. the "Great Fear."
 b. the "Great Panic."
 c. the "Great Riot."
 d. "Bastille Day."

_____ 3. The Declaration of the Rights of Man and of the Citizen embodied the revolutionary words
 a. "rights for all."
 b. "free citizens."
 c. "liberty, equality, fraternity."
 d. "one for all."

_____ 4. Olympe de Gouges led a protest for the
 a. rights of women.
 b. rights of serfs.
 c. right to hold titles.
 d. right to elect judges.

_____ 5. Nobles who lived in exile and hoped to restore the monarchy were known as
 a. refugees.
 b. home rulers.
 c. immigrants.
 d. émigrés.

_____ 6. The National Assembly divided France into 83 equal
 a. directories.
 b. departments.
 c. estates.
 d. states.

_____ 7. The Constitution of 1791 established
 a. an absolute monarchy.
 b. a federal system.
 c. a constitutional monarchy.
 d. a republic.

_____ 8. The moderates in the Legislative Assembly
 a. voted radical or conservative depending on the issue.
 b. voted to set up a republic.
 c. voted to keep the monarchy.
 d. did not vote.

_____ 9. The Legislative Assembly was forced into war after foreign powers sought to
 a. restore the monarchy.
 b. restore the estates.
 c. restore the Bastille.
 d. invade Canada.

_____ 10. Failure in war and economic shortages led to the takeover of the Commune and
 a. the Legislative Assembly.
 b. the National Assembly.
 c. a surrender to Prussia.
 d. suspension of the monarchy.

Name _____ Class _____ Date _____

Daily Quiz 21.3

Modern Chapter 12

The French Republic

MATCHING *(10 points each)* In the space provided, write the letter of the term or place that matches each description. Some answers will not be used.

_____ 1. voting rights for all men

_____ 2. republicans who favored dominance by Paris

_____ 3. leader of Jacobin radicals

_____ 4. military draft

_____ 5. against the Revolution

_____ 6. brutal Jacobin attempt to eliminate anyone suspected of disloyalty

_____ 7. leader of the Reign of Terror

_____ 8. government that replaced the National Convention

_____ 9. ambitious military leader

_____ 10. seizing power by force

a. conscription
b. National Convention
c. counterrevolutionary
d. Jacobins
e. Jean-Paul Marat
f. Maximilien Robespierre
g. the Directory
h. Napoléon Bonaparte
i. universal manhood suffrage
j. Georges-Jacques Danton
k. Reign of Terror
l. coup d'etat

Name _____ Class _____ Date _____

Modern Chapter 12

Daily Quiz 21.4

The Napoléonic Era

FILL IN THE BLANK *(10 points each)* For each of the following statements, fill in the blank with the appropriate word, phrase, or name.

_____ 1. Napoléon reorganized the government to give himself

_____ power.

_____ 2. A _____ means that people can vote *yes* or *no* but not suggest changes.

_____ 3. The _____ was a reorganization of all French law.

_____ 4. Under the Concordat, non-Catholics were allowed

_____.

_____ 5. In 1804, Napoléon was elected _____.

_____ 6. Napoléon attempted to invade Britain, but was defeated by

_____.

_____ 7. Opposition to Napoléon strengthened as the feeling of

_____ grew among conquered peoples.

_____ 8. The Russian army weakened Napoléon's forces by practicing a

_____ as they retreated.

_____ 9. The Hundred Days is the period when Louix XVIII was exiled and

_____ took power.

_____ 10. Napoléon's loss at Waterloo to British commander

_____ led to his final exile.

Name _____ Class _____ Date _____

 Daily Quiz 21.5

Modern Chapter 12 **A Return to Peace**

TRUE/FALSE Mark each statement *T* if it is true or *F* if it is false. If false explain why.

_____ 1. After Napoléon's defeat, European powers tried to uphold the Declaration of the Rights of Man and of the Citizen.

_____ 2. The Congress of Vienna met to resolve territorial questions and restore a balance of power.

_____ 3. The Congress of Vienna decided to follow the rule of legitimacy, or that all leaders should be elected in legitimate, fair elections.

_____ 4. Sweden was forced to give Norway to Denmark because of Sweden's collaboration with Napoléon.

_____ 5. Talleyrand, the English representative, helped resolve questions such as how to distribute land in Poland.

_____ 6. Reactionaries are people who always switch support to the winning side.

_____ 7. After the Napoléonic Era, European rulers governed conservatively and tried to suppress nationalist feeling.

_____ 8. The Holy Alliance was an agreement to restore the Holy Roman Empire.

_____ 9. Prince Metternich tried to ensure absolute rule by suppressing freedom of speech and the press.

_____ 10. Greek feelings of nationalism persisted, and rebellions led to independence for Greece.

Name _____ Class _____ Date _____

Daily Quiz 24.1

Modern Chapter 15

Liberal Reforms in Great Britain and Its Empire

MULTIPLE CHOICE *(10 points each)* For each of the following, write the letter of the best choice in the space provided.

_____ 1. The philosophy that supports government protection of individual rights and civil liberties is called
  a. protectionism.
  b. civil rights.
  c. liberalism.
  d. socialism.

_____ 2. The right to vote is known as
  a. a civil right.
  b. suffrage.
  c. liberalism.
  d. democracy.

_____ 3. The Reform Bill of 1832 helped the middle class
  a. clean up cities.
  b. obtain social services.
  c. gain a voice in government.
  d. pay less taxes.

_____ 4. As prime minister, Benjamin Disraeli was primarily interested in
  a. foreign affairs.
  b. domestic affairs.
  c. voting reforms.
  d. educational reforms.

_____ 5. A national education system was created during
  a. Disraeli's term.
  b. Gladstone's term.
  c. Peel's term.
  d. Asquith's term.

_____ 6. The "Irish question" dealt with Ireland's desire
  a. to have home rule.
  b. to join the British Empire.
  c. to have religious freedom.
  d. to split in half.

_____ 7. The Parliament Act of 1911 took away the power to veto tax bills from the
  a. House of Lords.
  b. House of Commons.
  c. monarch.
  d. prime minister.

_____ 8. Social reformers such as Emmeline Pankhurst fought for
  a. the abolition of slavery.
  b. a national health system.
  c. women's right to vote.
  d. workers' rights.

_____ 9. Recognizing past mistakes with colonies, Britain granted Canada
  a. representation in Parliament.
  b. tax relief.
  c. limited voting rights.
  d. self-government.

_____ 10. The Maori are
  a. native people of Australia.
  b. native people of New Zealand.
  c. British peace keeping troops.
  d. British island colonies.

Copyright © by Holt, Rinehart and Winston. All rights reserved.
World History: The Human Journey

Name _____ Class _____ Date _____

Daily Quiz 24.2

Modern Chapter 15 **Expansion and Reform in the United States**

FILL IN THE BLANK *(10 points each)* For each of the following statements, fill in the blank with the appropriate word, phrase, or name.

1. The _____ provided requirements for territories to gain statehood.

2. American expansion resulted in American Indians being _____.

3. Differing views among the three major regions of the United States led to _____.

4. The Civil War began in the United States after southern states _____ from the Union.

5. _____ meant that armies aggressively tried to destroy military and civilian resources.

6. The _____ freed slaves in the United States.

7. New, sparsely populated states had _____ voting restrictions.

8. Increased numbers of voters changed elections; for example, candidates were selected by _____, rather than a small group of legislators.

9. Lucretia Mott and Elizabeth Cady Stanton led the fight for _____.

10. Population growth and diversity was stimulated by _____.

Name _____ Class _____ Date _____

Daily Quiz 24.3

Modern Chapter 15 **Revolution and Reform in France**

MATCHING *(10 points each)* In the space provided, write the letter of the term or place that matches each description. Some answers will not be used.

_____ 1. ruler who favored the conservative upper middle class

_____ 2. socialist-influenced government that took hold after the revolution of 1848

_____ 3. first president elected by Second French Republic

_____ 4. authoritarian regime run by Napoléon III

_____ 5. costly conflict with Russia

_____ 6. resulted in the Prussian and German defeat of France

_____ 7. Parisian group that favored socialist reforms for French government

_____ 8. created the Constitution of 1875

_____ 9. against all forms of government

_____ 10. falsely accused army captain whose case divided republicans and conservatives

a. Second French Empire
b. Communards
c. Florence Nightingale
d. Louis Philippe, the "citizen king"
e. Treaty of Frankfurt
f. Louis-Napoléon
g. Franco-Prussian War
h. Crimean War
i. Second French Republic
j. Alfred Dreyfus
k. anarchists
l. Third Republic

Name _____ Class _____ Date _____

Modern Chapter 15

Daily Quiz 24.4

Latin Americans Win Independence

TRUE/FALSE Mark each statement *T* if it is true or *F* if it is false. If false explain why.

_____ 1. Portuguese and Spanish colonies in Latin America were given the right to free trade.

_____ 2. Haciendas and *fazendas* were small, shabby peasant towns.

_____ 3. Peninsulares were people born in Spain or Portugal.

_____ 4. Mestizos were white people born in the colonies.

_____ 5. Toussaint-Louverture led mulattoes and slaves, successfully revolted against Spanish settlers, and established the country of Haiti.

_____ 6. General Agustín de Iturbide led a Mexican peasant army into an ultimately unsuccessful revolt against Spain.

_____ 7. Simón Bolívar's fight to free Venezuela was the "beginning of the end" for the Spanish Empire in Latin America.

_____ 8. Spain's attempts to regain its colonies led President Monroe to declare that the United States would not help European nations take back colonies.

_____ 9. Unification of Latin countries was hampered by divisions between upper-class creoles and conservative mestizos.

_____ 10. *Caudillos* were ambitious mestizo military leaders who ruled as dictators.

Name _____ Class _____ Date _____

Modern Chapter 16

Daily Quiz 25.1

The Unification of Italy

FILL IN THE BLANK *(10 points each)* For each of the following statements, fill in the blank with the appropriate word, phrase, or name.

1. The nationalist movement of the early 1800s was known as _____.

2. Secret nationalist societies, such as the _____, formed.

3. Giuseppe Mazzini stated that a _____, not a pope or king, should rule Italy.

4. The _____ called for Italian patriots to join and spread nationalist ideas.

5. Some conservative nationalists called for rule by _____.

6. As chief minister, _____ governed the kingdom of Sardinia and supported liberal republican goals.

7. In an effort to achieve unity, Camillo Benso di Cavour and _____ united to drive Austria from the states of Lombardy and Venetia.

8. States kept by Austria after the war revolted and voted to join _____.

9. _____ led the drive to unite the southern half of Italy and Sicily.

10. By 1870, the Italian states, including the Austrian ones, united under _____.

Name _____ Class _____ Date _____

Modern Chapter 16

Daily Quiz 25.2

The Unification of Germany

MULTIPLE CHOICE *(10 points each)* For each of the following, write the letter of the best choice in the space provided.

_____ 1. When the Congress of Vienna created the German Confederation, it gave more territory and power to
   a. Germany.
   b. Prussia.
   c. Austria.
   d. Saxony.

_____ 2. A rising sense of nationalism made German states prefer Prussia to
   a. Austria.
   b. Russia.
   c. Rome.
   d. Russia.

_____ 3. Aristocratic landowners who led the complaints against Prussian taxes were known as
   a. Junkers.
   b. Zollverein.
   c. Nationalists.
   d. Free Traders.

_____ 4. The customs union that helped create economic unity in the German states was known as
   a. Junkers.
   b. Zollverein.
   c. German Economic Union.
   d. German Customs Union.

_____ 5. Bismarck provoked Austria into war through the ongoing dispute over former
   a. Italian territories.
   b. Danish territories.
   c. Russian territories.
   d. Prussian territories.

_____ 6. Bismarck demonstrated Prussia's military power during the
   a. Danish War.
   b. Napoléonic Wars.
   c. Crimean War.
   d. Seven Weeks' War.

_____ 7. The Treaty of Prague resulted in the formation of the
   a. North German Confederation.
   b. German Confederation.
   c. Prussian Confederaton.
   d. Danish Confederation.

_____ 8. Bismarck waged the Franco-Prussian War in order to
   a. win back Venetia.
   b. destroy Austria.
   c. win the support of France.
   d. win the support of southern Germany.

_____ 9. The German Empire was ruled by a kaiser, who was
   a. a president.
   b. a chief minister.
   c. a limited monarch.
   d. an emperor.

_____ 10. The Reichstag was made up of elected members, but compared to the Bundesrat, the Reichstag had
   a. limited power.
   b. total power.
   c. equal power.
   d. great influence.

Copyright © by Holt, Rinehart and Winston. All rights reserved.

Name _____ Class _____ Date _____

Daily Quiz 25.3

Modern Chapter 16

Opposition to Bismarck

TRUE/FALSE Mark each statement *T* if it is true or *F* if it is false. If false explain why.

_____ 1. Bismarck's biggest challenge came from a new politically powerful middle class.

_____ 2. The Centre Party was primarily made up of Catholics.

_____ 3. Kulturkampf was a program aimed at unifying the cultures of southern and northern Germany.

_____ 4. The German Industrial Revolution benefited from the lessons of British and French industrialization.

_____ 5. German economic power was slowed by the formation of cartels.

_____ 6. The Social Democratic Party fought for the rights of workers by voting against government ownership of industry.

_____ 7. Strict laws against freedom of press and speech helped reduce the power of the Social Democrats.

_____ 8. To prevent the growth of a difficult socialist movement, Bismarck granted some government-directed social reforms.

_____ 9. William II supported a limited constitutional monarchy.

_____ 10. Working with Bismarck, William II made Germany into a military and industrial power.

Daily Quiz 25.4

Modern Chapter 16 — Reform and Revolution in Russia

MATCHING *(10 points each)* In the space provided, write the letter of the term or place that matches each description. Some answers will not be used.

_____ 1. ruler with absolute power

_____ 2. program to force non-Russians to adopt Russian culture and language

_____ 3. union of all Slavic people under Russian leadership

_____ 4. reform-minded czar

_____ 5. legislation that freed serfs

_____ 6. group supporting overthrow of existing political, social, and economic structure

_____ 7. radical terrorist group that assassinated Alexander II

_____ 8. violent massacre of Jews

_____ 9. political party supported by workers

_____ 10. ineffective post-revolutionary parliament

a. People's Will
b. Alexander II
c. autocrat
d. nihilists
e. Emancipation Edict
f. Pan-Slavism
g. Duma
h. "Russification"
i. *zemstvo*
j. pogroms
k. Social Democratic Labor Party
l. October Manifesto

Name _____ Class _____ Date _____

Modern Chapter 16

Daily Quiz 25.5

Unrest in Austria-Hungary

MULTIPLE CHOICE *(10 points each)* For each of the following, write the letter of the best choice in the space provided.

_____ 1. Revolutions in many European countries were inspired by
   a. the revolt in France.
   b. the revolt in the United States.
   c. economic changes.
   d. reform in Britain.

_____ 2. Many people under the rule of the Austrian Empire were
   a. Austrians.
   b. Russians.
   c. Italians.
   d. Magyars.

_____ 3. Lajos Kossuth led a revolution to free
   a. Hungary.
   b. Finland.
   c. the Ukraine.
   d. Austria.

_____ 4. The Dual Monarchy gave Hungary some independence by giving it a separate
   a. president.
   b. emperor.
   c. parliament.
   d. tariff system.

_____ 5. Austria's loss in the Seven Weeks' War made it try to rebuild its empire in
   a. Central Asia.
   b. Russia.
   c. the Ukraine.
   d. the Balkans.

_____ 6. Russia wanted control of the Balkans to gain access to
   a. the Mediterranean.
   b. the Indian Ocean.
   c. Africa.
   d. Asia.

_____ 7. Russia gained control of Bulgaria from the
   a. Treaty of Prague.
   b. Treaty of San Stefano.
   c. Treaty of Romania.
   d. Treaty of Serbia.

_____ 8. To lessen Russian influence, the Congress of Berlin reduced the size of
   a. Romania.
   b. Serbia.
   c. Moscow.
   d. Bulgaria.

_____ 9. Austria defied the Congress of Berlin by annexing
   a. Serbia.
   b. Romania.
   c. Bosnia and Bulgaria.
   d. Bosnia and Herzegovina.

_____ 10. The realignment of borders and powers left Austria with a new enemy—
   a. Serbia.
   b. Bulgaria.
   c. Hungary.
   d. Greece.

Copyright © by Holt, Rinehart and Winston. All rights reserved.

World History: The Human Journey

Name _____ Class _____ Date _____

Modern Chapter 17

Daily Quiz 26.1

The Roots of Western Imperialism

TRUE/FALSE Mark each statement *T* if it is true or *F* if it is false. If false explain why.

_____ 1. Imperialism in the 19th century led to a concentration of power by the early 20th century.

_____ 2. Nationalism was the root of imperialistic action during the late 1800s and early 1900s.

_____ 3. A settlement colony is an area where a few European officials rule over the native people.

_____ 4. A sphere of influence is an area where one nation has a special interest.

_____ 5. Nationalist feeling had little effect on larger, more powerful countries.

_____ 6. Imperialist nations created feelings of pride among colonized people.

_____ 7. Industrialism forced an empire to concentrate on creating jobs and materials within its ruling country.

_____ 8. Rapid population growth caused many Europeans to emigrate to the colonies to find jobs.

_____ 9. European colonists felt that it was their duty to help colonies maintain their cultural identity.

_____ 10. Christian missionaries were not able to exert much influence in many non-Western colonies.

Name _____ Class _____ Date _____

CHAPTER 26

Modern Chapter 17

Daily Quiz 26.2

European Claims in North Africa

MULTIPLE CHOICE *(10 points each)* For each of the following, write the letter of the best choice in the space provided.

_____ 1. Algeria was overtaken by the
   a. British.
   b. Spanish.
   c. French.
   d. Italians.

_____ 2. Under French rule, Tunis was a
   a. settlement colony.
   b. protectorate.
   c. dependent colony.
   d. sphere of influence.

_____ 3. Under a 1904 agreement, northern Morocco became a
   a. Spanish sphere of influence.
   b. Spanish protectorate.
   c. French protectorate.
   d. British colony.

_____ 4. Part of Egypt's economic problems came from
   a. building an army.
   b. building the Suez Canal.
   c. building the Strait of Gibraltar.
   d. war with Turkey.

_____ 5. Britain took control of the Suez Canal to gain access to
   a. Britain's colonies.
   b. new trade routes in Africa.
   c. the Northwest Passage.
   d. China.

_____ 6. The establishment of a committee to oversee Egypt's finances led to
   a. economic stability for Egypt.
   b. French control of Egypt.
   c. civil war in Egypt.
   d. rebellion in Egypt.

_____ 7. The British wanted control of the Sudan to
   a. build canals on the Suez.
   b. build dams on the Nile.
   c. gain access to India.
   d. gain access to the Red Sea.

_____ 8. In 1881, the people of the Sudan rebelled against Egyptian rule and were led by the
   a. Mahdi.
   b. Khan.
   c. Khartoum.
   d. Sultan.

_____ 9. The Fashoda crisis was a standoff between France and
   a. Egypt.
   b. Spain.
   c. Britain.
   d. Algiers.

_____ 10. Control of the Sudan went to
   a. France.
   b. Britain.
   c. France and Egypt.
   d. Britain and Egypt.

Name _____ Class _____ Date _____

CHAPTER 26

Modern Chapter 17

Daily Quiz 26.3

European Claims in Sub-Saharan Africa

MATCHING *(10 points each)* In the space provided, write the letter of the term or place that matches each description. Some answers will not be used.

_____ 1. Senegalese who fought against the French

_____ 2. journalist hired by the *New York Herald* to find Dr. David Livingstone

_____ 3. Belgian king who ruled over Congo as a private fiefdom

_____ 4. descendants of Dutch settlers in South Africa

_____ 5. language developed by settlers in South Africa

_____ 6. Zulu leader who fought the Boers

_____ 7. British fight to gain control of the Transvaal government

_____ 8. governing as if a colony is not able to take care of itself

_____ 9. Ethiopian ruler who fought Italian colonization

_____ 10. giving up a native culture to blend in with another

a. Samory Touré
b. King Leopold II
c. Afrikaans
d. paternalism
e. assimilation
f. Henry Stanley
g. Boers
h. Gold Coast
i. Shaka
j. Liberia
k. Boer War
l. Menelik II

Name _____ Class _____ Date _____

Modern Chapter **17**

Daily Quiz 26.4
Expansion in Asia

TRUE/FALSE Mark each statement *T* if it is true or *F* if it is false. If false explain why.

_____ 1. The British East India Company controlled much of India throughout the early to mid-1800s.

_____ 2. British society and the Indian upper classes often mixed in social events.

_____ 3. British schools in India taught Western ideas and beliefs.

_____ 4. Indian Muslims believed that British rule helped to protect them from violence.

_____ 5. After the Meiji Restoration, the Japanese class system became more rigid.

_____ 6. In an effort to modernize quickly, Japan copied many Western ideas and institutions.

_____ 7. In the Sino-Japanese War, Japan fought China over independence for Vietnam.

_____ 8. Siam's clever diplomatic maneuvers enabled it to remain independent of European rule.

_____ 9. War over the Samoa Islands was avoided when Germany withdrew its interest.

_____ 10. The United States removed Spanish control from the Philippines, then defeated Filipinos fighting for independence.

Name _____ Class _____ Date _____

Modern Chapter 17

Daily Quiz 26.5

Imperialism in Latin America

MULTIPLE CHOICE *(10 points each)* For each of the following, write the letter of the best choice in the space provided.

_____ 1. Outside investments in Latin American countries did not help Latin Americans because
   a. business was bad.
   b. the market was poor.
   c. the profits left the countries.
   d. investments were managed poorly.

_____ 2. Latin American countries weakened themselves by
   a. pursuing wars.
   b. taking loans they could not repay.
   c. imposing heavy tariffs.
   d. making bad investments.

_____ 3. The Spanish-American War was sparked by
   a. tension between Cuba and Spain.
   b. tariff disputes.
   c. American attacks on Spain.
   d. Spain's blockade of Cuba.

_____ 4. The Treaty of Paris forced Spain to give up Cuba, and gave
   a. Puerto Rico to the United States.
   b. Puerto Rico to Spain.
   c. freedom to the Philippines.
   d. Guam to Spain.

_____ 5. The Platt Amendment allowed the United States to
   a. run the Cuban government.
   b. intervene in Spanish colonies.
   c. intervene in Cuba.
   d. disarm Cuba.

_____ 6. To get land in Colombia for a canal, the United States
   a. helped Panamanian rebels.
   b. attacked Colombia.
   c. overthrew the Colombian government.
   d. attacked Spain.

_____ 7. Carlos Juan Finlay helped with the construction of the Panama Canal by
   a. brokering a lease with Colombia.
   b. leading Panamanian rebels.
   c. designing the canal.
   d. discovering the cause of yellow fever.

_____ 8. The Roosevelt Corollary said that the United States would ensure that Latin American countries would
   a. put down rebellions.
   b. pay export tariffs.
   c. repay loans.
   d. not build armies.

_____ 9. Venustiano Carranza and Emiliano Zapata led revolts in
   a. Panama.
   b. Mexico.
   c. Colombia.
   d. Nicaragua.

_____ 10. President Wilson sent troops to Mexico when
   a. Carranza led a revolt.
   b. Zapata voiced demands from peasants.
   c. war started in Europe.
   d. Villa raided Columbus, New Mexico.

Name _____ Class _____ Date _____

Modern Chapter 18

Daily Quiz 27.1

Setting the Stage for War

TRUE/FALSE Mark each statement *T* if it is true or *F* if it is false. If false explain why.

_____ 1. Conflict arose in Europe when people began to align themselves according to ethnicity rather than borders.

_____ 2. European nations were concerned about building new industries and therefore neglected their military.

_____ 3. Bismarck formed the Triple Alliance in an effort to isolate Russia diplomatically.

_____ 4. The Triple Entente was sparked by Britain's fear of Russia's naval power.

_____ 5. The Balkans were important to other European countries because the Balkans could provide access to the Mediterranean Sea.

_____ 6. The alliance between Britain and Russia was disrupted by their disagreement over Germany's attempts to expand into the East through Constantinople.

_____ 7. Austria-Hungary sought the support of Germany because it feared Britain would aid the Serbs.

_____ 8. Austria-Hungary declared war on Serbia after Serbia ignored the Austro-Hungarian ultimatum.

_____ 9. Germany declared war on France before France could mobilize to support Russia.

_____ 10. Britain felt compelled to declare war on Germany after it ignored Italy's declaration of neutrality.

Copyright © by Holt, Rinehart and Winston. All rights reserved.

Name _____ Class _____ Date _____

Modern Chapter 18

Daily Quiz 27.2

World War I: A New Kind of War

MULTIPLE CHOICE *(10 points each)* For each of the following, write the letter of the best choice in the space provided.

_____ 1. The Central Powers consisted of Germany, Austria-Hungary, the Ottoman Empire, and
   a. Serbia.
   b. Greece.
   c. Bulgaria.
   d. Belgium.

_____ 2. World War I differed from other wars because it was
   a. vast in scope.
   b. industrialized.
   c. a guerilla war.
   d. fought on the ocean.

_____ 3. The Central Powers were able to affect Allied shipping through the use of
   a. U-boats.
   b. machine guns.
   c. better sea mapping.
   d. control of Middle Eastern ports.

_____ 4. World War I was the first war in which
   a. photography was important.
   b. airplanes were used.
   c. nuclear weapons were used.
   d. spies were important.

_____ 5. Because so many men went to fight in the war, factories employed
   a. women.
   b. children.
   c. very young men.
   d. the clergy.

_____ 6. Propaganda was used to
   a. build trenches.
   b. poison soldiers.
   c. build patriotism.
   d. protect women and children.

_____ 7. The disaster at Gallipoli was sparked by the Allies' attempt to
   a. gain access to China.
   b. capture Constantinople.
   c. gain access to the Balkans.
   d. capture Troy.

_____ 8. A war of attrition is one fought
   a. with new technology.
   b. with constant diplomatic contact.
   c. by trying to outlast each other.
   d. with stealth.

_____ 9. The United States was enraged by
   a. Germany's attempt to ally with Mexico.
   b. Germany's attempt to ally with Cuba.
   c. Latin-American support of Germany.
   d. German spies in the United States.

_____ 10. The United States was persuaded to join the war because of its trade connections with the Allies and its
   a. dislike of the kaiser.
   b. nationalist feeling.
   c. aim for European expansion.
   d. belief in democracy.

Name _____ Class _____ Date _____

CHAPTER 27
Modern Chapter 18

Daily Quiz 27.3
The Russian Revolution

FILL IN THE BLANK *(10 points each)* For each of the following statements, fill in the blank with the appropriate word, phrase, or name.

1. Russia's army, roads, and weapons were _____ for war.

2. The czar _____ the Duma when it demanded government reforms.

3. The czar was unable to put down demonstrations because he did not have the support of the _____.

4. The word *soviet* means _____.

5. The Petrograd Soviets believed that political equality should also mean _____.

6. The provisional government angered the soviets because it decided to _____ the war.

7. The Bolsheviks overthrew the provisional government, dissolved the assembly, and took control, renaming themselves the _____.

8. The revolutionaries angered the Allies by _____.

9. Division between the Whites, who supported the return of the monarchy, and the _____, who did not, dragged on for three years.

10. Russia was eventually renamed _____.

Name _____ Class _____ Date _____

Daily Quiz 27.4

Modern Chapter 18

The Terms of Peace

MULTIPLE CHOICE *(10 points each)* For each of the following, write the letter of the best choice in the space provided.

_____ 1. The Fourteen Points was
   a. France's strategy in Russia.
   b. a Russian battlefield.
   c. a Belgian peace treaty.
   d. Wilson's postwar plan.

_____ 2. One of President Wilson's ideas was
   a. U.S. control of the Balkans.
   b. U.S. takeover of Russia.
   c. freedom of the seas for all nations.
   d. more power to imperials.

_____ 3. President Wilson called for the establishment of
   a. a world police force.
   b. further trade barriers.
   c. a general association of nations.
   d. a stronger U.S. army.

_____ 4. Germany's withdrawal of troops from the eastern front was part of the
   a. Treaty of Alsace-Lorraine.
   b. Treaty of Brest Litovsk.
   c. Treaty of Paris.
   d. Treaty of Versailles.

_____ 5. The Central Powers were dealt a heavy blow by
   a. Russia's return to the Allies.
   b. France's use of U-boats.
   c. the fall of the Red Army.
   d. the split of Austria-Hungary.

_____ 6. President Wilson's demands for peace included a German government that
   a. represented the German people.
   b. represented Bulgaria.
   c. renounced socialism.
   d. could control Russia.

_____ 7. Germany was required to
   a. turn over its arms.
   b. turn over its leaders.
   c. drop trade barriers.
   d. agree to Russian control.

_____ 8. The Paris Peace Conference angered some because it was
   a. dominated by the Allies.
   b. dominated by the Russians.
   c. dominated by the Habsburgs.
   d. held in secret.

_____ 9. President Wilson proposed a League of Nations, which would keep
   a. a standing army.
   b. the economy stable.
   c. governments stable.
   d. world peace.

_____ 10. President Wilson worried that punishing any nation too harshly would lead to
   a. economic chaos.
   b. unstable government.
   c. anger in the United States.
   d. future war.

Copyright © by Holt, Rinehart and Winston. All rights reserved.
World History: The Human Journey

CHAPTER 27

Daily Quiz 27.5

Modern Chapter 18

Creating a "New" Europe

TRUE/FALSE Mark each statement *T* if it is true or *F* if it is false. If false explain why.

_____ 1. The Allied Powers signed treaties with each of the former Central Powers.

_____ 2. The Treaty of Versailles was designed to punish Austria and Hungary.

_____ 3. The Central Powers were angered at having to share the payment of reparations to the Allies.

_____ 4. Polish independence was one of the results of the Treaty of Versailles.

_____ 5. The Allies set up a task force to make sure Germany did not rearm.

_____ 6. The Treaty of Versailles assembled several small German states and created the nation of Yugoslavia.

_____ 7. When the new boundaries did not fit natural ethnic divisions, genocide was sometimes the result.

_____ 8. The League of Nations was made up of an assembly, a secretariat, and a world bank.

_____ 9. The League of Nations agreed not to interfere with the new governments of former colonies.

_____ 10. The United States did not join the League of Nations because Wilson felt it did not give the United States enough power.

Name _____ Class _____ Date _____

Modern Chapter **19**

Daily Quiz 28.1
The Postwar Era

MATCHING *(10 points each)* In the space provided, write the letter of the term or place that matches each description. Some answers will not be used.

_____ 1. killed an estimated 20 million people

_____ 2. idea that no one set of principles is good for all groups

_____ 3. group of writers who wrote after World War I and expressed the disillusionment of the era

_____ 4. conscious and unconscious ideas brought together in a dreamlike way

_____ 5. revolutionary composer

_____ 6. free-form musical style developed from a blend of cultures

_____ 7. art form that features geometric designs and shows an object from different viewpoints at the same time

_____ 8. architect who designed buildings to fit their environment

_____ 9. modern young women who started wearing short hair and skirts

_____ 10. ban on alcoholic beverages

a. prohibition
b. international style
c. functionalism
d. influenza pandemic
e. cubism
f. Igor Stravinsky
g. moral relativism
h. surrealism
i. Frank Lloyd Wright
j. flappers
k. Lost Generation
l. jazz

CHAPTER 28

Daily Quiz 28.2
Postwar Prosperity Crumbles

FILL IN THE BLANK *(10 points each)* For each of the following statements, fill in the blank with the appropriate word, phrase, or name.

1. Agricultural expansion during World War I led to _____ for farmers in the postwar era.

2. Economic nationalism means limiting trade in order to _____.

3. _____ made it difficult for Europeans to sell goods in America, which then prevented Europeans from paying their debts.

4. The strength of the stock market in the 1920s lead to an increase in _____, or risky investments.

5. The stock market crashed on Black Tuesday because people rushed to sell stocks for wildly _____ prices.

6. The Great Depression was the result of the _____.

7. France was able to stave off the effects of the Great Depression temporarily because it was less _____.

8. The United States was unable to help people because of a lack of _____.

9. President Franklin D. Roosevelt instituted a plan of social programs called the _____.

10. The _____ provided for unemployment and old-age benefits.

Name _____ Class _____ Date _____

CHAPTER 28

Modern Chapter 19

Daily Quiz 28.3

Political Tensions After World War I

MULTIPLE CHOICE *(10 points each)* For each of the following, write the letter of the best choice in the space provided.

_____ 1. One of the effects the war had on France was
   a. a heavy debt.
   b. increased exports.
   c. improved farming methods.
   d. dissent with Britain.

_____ 2. The Maginot Line was meant to
   a. improve rail transportation.
   b. improve communication.
   c. protect France from Germany.
   d. protect France from Austria.

_____ 3. Several nations agreed to settle disputes peacefully, as outlined in the
   a. Maginot Line.
   b. Treaty of Paris.
   c. Treaty of Locarno.
   d. Locarno Pact.

_____ 4. To achieve their political goals, workers across France called for a general strike, or a
   a. new vote.
   b. refusal to work.
   c. refusal to vote.
   d. tax protest.

_____ 5. The Popular Front was a
   a. left-wing government.
   b. right-wing government.
   c. dictatorship.
   d. right-wing police force.

_____ 6. Nationalization means that an industry is
   a. under government control.
   b. a domestic cartel.
   c. unable to export goods.
   d. run by a national union.

_____ 7. Britain slowly recovered, because of a reform-minded coalition between the Liberal Party and the
   a. Labour Party.
   b. Conservative Party.
   c. Workers' Party.
   d. Unionist Party.

_____ 8. The Easter Rising was a revolt led by
   a. Scottish nationalists.
   b. British nationalists.
   c. British communists.
   d. Irish nationalists.

_____ 9. Irish demands for independence resulted in a
   a. peace agreement.
   b. general strike.
   c. divided north and south.
   d. complete loss of independence.

_____ 10. Economic problems and cultural divides resulted in
   a. instability in Eastern Europe.
   b. Irish civil war.
   c. Russian democracy.
   d. unity in Eastern Europe.

Daily Quiz 28.4

Modern Chapter 19 **Fascist Dictatorships in Italy and Germany**

TRUE/FALSE Mark each statement *T* if it is true or *F* if it is false. If false explain why.

_____ 1. Benito Mussolini's views switched from mild socialism to a strict form of communism.

_____ 2. Fascism appeals to the lower classes because of its emphasis on preservation of class and property.

_____ 3. The Black Shirts enforced fascism by attacking socialist movements.

_____ 4. Mussolini rose to power by appealing to the peoples' fear of monarchy.

_____ 5. Mussolini's rule could be described as a police state.

_____ 6. Germany's discontent arose from economic difficulties and embarrassment over the Treaty of Versailles.

_____ 7. Hitler's ideas appealed to both the upper classes and the communists.

_____ 8. Hitler rose to power on his promise that Germany could re-emerge as an economic rather than military power.

_____ 9. Hitler's promise of a master race meant a classless society in which the brightest and most talented people could rise to the top.

_____ 10. Hitler's placement of troops in the Rhineland raised immediate worries in the rest of Europe.

Daily Quiz 28.5

Modern Chapter 19 — **Dictatorship in the Soviet Union**

FILL IN THE BLANK *(10 points each)* For each of the following statements, fill in the blank with the appropriate word, phrase, or name.

1. The policy known as _____ nationalized Russian industries.

2. Economic collapse led Lenin to institute the New Economic Policy, which allowed for some _____ for private citizens.

3. _____ allowed peasants to share farmland and equipment.

4. Trotsky believed that communism called for a worldwide _____.

5. _____ promoted the idea that a successful revolution in one country would lead to other successful revolutions.

6. _____ meant that the government controlled all economic decisions.

7. The Five-Year Plan increased some industrial production, but caused hardship by decreasing production of _____.

8. The _____ of the Communist Party held the power in the Soviet government.

9. Stalin's _____ aimed to eliminate all party members perceived as disloyal.

10. The Comintern's goal was to _____.

Name _____ Class _____ Date _____

Modern Chapter 20

Daily Quiz 29.1
The British Empire in the Postwar Era

MULTIPLE CHOICE *(10 points each)* For each of the following, write the letter of the best choice in the space provided.

_____ 1. The Wafd Party wanted
  a. Ethiopian independence.
  b. Egyptian independence.
  c. Sudanese independence.
  d. Indian independence.

_____ 2. The Anglo-Egyptian Treaty was prompted by
  a. Italy's invasion of Ethiopia.
  b. Italy's invasion of Egypt.
  c. Egypt's invasion of Italy.
  d. Italy's invasion of the Suez.

_____ 3. Despite a treaty, Egyptians remained angered by British
  a. support of Ethiopia.
  b. support of Italy.
  c. trade restrictions.
  d. military presence.

_____ 4. The effort to build a Jewish state in Palestine was known as
  a. Semitism.
  b. Zionism.
  c. nationalism.
  d. Judaism.

_____ 5. British support of a Jewish state came to be known as the
  a. British-Judeo agreement.
  b. Jewish-Arab Declaration.
  c. Balfour Declaration.
  d. British Declaration.

_____ 6. Tensions in Palestine arose out of Britain's
  a. military presence.
  b. attempt to please both Jews and Arabs.
  c. control of the Suez Canal.
  d. fascist rule.

_____ 7. Decisions about Indian independence from Britain divided
  a. Indians.
  b. British.
  c. British and Indians.
  d. Indian Muslims.

_____ 8. Mohandas Gandhi led the drive for Indian independence using
  a. nonviolent methods.
  b. violent methods.
  c. guerilla tactics.
  d. libel.

_____ 9. Britain's harsh reaction to Gandhi's efforts
  a. put down rebellion.
  b. created violence.
  c. turned moderate Indians against the British.
  d. raised nationalist feeling in Britain.

_____ 10. The British Commonwealth of Nations
  a. created an economic link between France and Great Britain.
  b. established a defensive alliance among nations.
  c. granted partial independence to British dominions.
  d. caused discontent and revolt among British dominions.

Name _____ Class _____ Date _____

Modern Chapter 20

Daily Quiz 29.2

Turkey, Persia, and Africa

TRUE/FALSE Mark each statement *T* if it is true or *F* if it is false. If false explain why.

_____ 1. After World War I, the Ottoman Empire sent troops to Greece to regain territory.

_____ 2. Mustafa Kemal installed a government with a president and two political parties.

_____ 3. Kemal felt the Turks could make more progress if Islam were separated from the government.

_____ 4. Kemal's reforms were based on maintaining a strong cultural identity.

_____ 5. Kemal's reforms led to economic instability.

_____ 6. Military leader Reza Khan deposed the shah and took control of Persia.

_____ 7. As shah, Reza Shah Pahlavi sought to modernize Iran.

_____ 8. In an effort to balance Russian and German influences, Iran sought an alliance with Britain.

_____ 9. Western education discouraged African nationalists from seeking independence.

_____ 10. By the 1930s Africans were increasingly dissatisfied with a lack of independence.

Copyright © by Holt, Rinehart and Winston. All rights reserved.

Name _____ Class _____ Date _____

Modern Chapter **20**

Daily Quiz 29.3

Unrest in China

FILL IN THE BLANK *(10 points each)* For each of the following statements, fill in the blank with the appropriate word, phrase, or name.

1. The _____ was a plan to give all nations trade rights to China.

2. Empress Dowager Tz'u-hsi blocked attempts at _____.

3. The Boxer Rebellion was an _____ movement.

4. Led by Sun Yixian, the _____ was a reform-minded, nationalist party.

5. Chinese nationalists believed that China had to _____ to protect itself economically from foreign control.

6. Sun Yixian's "Three Principles Of the People" called for democracy and equal rights, economic improvements, and _____.

7. China's request for foreign aid was answered only by _____.

8. _____ led the conservative branch of the Nationalists, and created a dictatorship.

9. The Long March was a Nationalist drive to remove _____.

10. Mao Zedong's support was based on his recruitment of Chinese _____.

Name _____ Class _____ Date _____

Modern Chapter 20

Daily Quiz 29.4
Imperialism in Japan

MULTIPLE CHOICE *(10 points each)* For each of the following, write the letter of the best choice in the space provided.

_____ 1. Japan wanted to expand its territory to
   a. protect itself from outsiders.
   b. make room for its large population.
   c. threaten China.
   d. show western nations its progress.

_____ 2. Japan and Britain formed an alliance to protect their interests from
   a. China.
   b. Russia.
   c. Manchuria.
   d. Germany.

_____ 3. Japan sought to remove Russia from
   a. Korea.
   b. Manchuria.
   c. Beijing.
   d. Taiwan.

_____ 4. Japanese victories against the Russians displayed Japanese
   a. wealth.
   b. air force.
   c. naval power.
   d. intelligence network.

_____ 5. The Treaty of Portsmouth gave Japan dominance in
   a. Manchuria.
   b. China.
   c. Korea.
   d. the Baltic Sea.

_____ 6. Japanese population increases led to
   a. famine.
   b. disease.
   c. emigration.
   d. military strength.

_____ 7. Japan was angered by the United States's
   a. military presence.
   b. high tariffs.
   c. immigration policy.
   d. naval attacks.

_____ 8. The Japanese expansion was threatened by
   a. a small labor force.
   b. lack of raw materials.
   c. political unrest.
   d. an emphasis on the military.

_____ 9. The 1929 collapse of world markets led Japan to question
   a. agricultural economies.
   b. expansion.
   c. imperialism.
   d. westernization.

_____ 10. Japan's military victories led to
   a. increased militarism.
   b. pacificist feeling.
   c. increased immigration.
   d. fear of military leadership.

Copyright © by Holt, Rinehart and Winston. All rights reserved.

Name _____ Class _____ Date _____

Daily Quiz 29.5

Modern Chapter **20** **Latin America Between the Wars**

TRUE/FALSE Mark each statement *T* if it is true or *F* if it is false. If false explain why.

_____ 1. Mining and oil industries in Latin America were owned primarily by Latin American countries.

_____ 2. Lack of foreign investment and power sources hurt Latin American industrialism.

_____ 3. Labor unions with anarchic or socialist beliefs often used general strikes to make their demands.

_____ 4. Economic prosperity led to democracy and government stability.

_____ 5. Working-class concerns helped Diego Rivera rise to political power in Mexico.

_____ 6. Latin American exports maintained strength during the worldwide depression of the 1930s.

_____ 7. Political and economic unrest led to takeovers by authoritarian governments.

_____ 8. Roosevelt's Good Neighbor Policy called for U.S. intervention in Mexican political crises.

_____ 9. The stability of Fulgencio Batista's government caused the United States to cancel the Platt Amendment.

_____ 10. Mexico's dependence on foreign-owned oil companies hindered attempts at independence.

CHAPTER 30

Modern Chapter 21

Daily Quiz 30.1

Threats to World Peace

FILL IN THE BLANK *(10 points each)* For each of the following statements, fill in the blank with the appropriate word, phrase, or name.

1. The Kellogg-Briand Pact was supposed to make war _____.

2. The assassination of liberal Japanese prime minister Osachi Hamaguchi led to a _____ takeover.

3. Japanese attacks on _____ were only punished by a condemnation from the League of Nations.

4. The League of Nations did not aid _____ when Italy threatened it.

5. _____ had little effect on Italy, and few countries tried to enforce them.

6. _____ uprisings against socialist reforms led to the Spanish Civil War.

7. _____, or Republicans, supported the government and reforms.

8. Spanish Nationalists received the support of other _____ regimes, Germany and Italy.

9. The _____, made up of volunteers from France, Great Britain, and the United States, fought for the Loyalists.

10. Defeat of the Loyalists made Francisco Franco the leader of a _____.

Name _____ Class _____ Date _____

Modern Chapter 21

Daily Quiz 30.2
Hitler's Aggressions

MULTIPLE CHOICE *(10 points each)* For each of the following, write the letter of the best choice in the space provided.

_____ 1. The Axis Powers' Anti-Comintern Pact was a pledge to fight
   a. fascism.
   b. communism.
   c. the Allies.
   d. the U.S.

_____ 2. Germany's annexation of Austria was a violation of the
   a. Anti-Comintern Pact.
   b. Treaty of Paris.
   c. Congress of Vienna.
   d. Treaty of Versailles.

_____ 3. The League of Nations responded to Hitler's move into Austria by
   a. setting economic sanctions.
   b. issuing a warning.
   c. doing nothing.
   d. sending troops to Germany.

_____ 4. Hitler wanted to annex the Sudetenland because of its
   a. defenselessness.
   b. German citizens.
   c. alliance with France.
   d. border with Italy.

_____ 5. At the Munich Conference, Neville Chamberlain and Édouard Daladier agreed to
   a. Hitler's annexation of the Sudetenland.
   b. Italy's alliance with Germany.
   c. disarm Britain and France.
   d. protect Czechoslovakia.

_____ 6. Appeasement means to
   a. reach a peace agreement.
   b. negotiate a treaty.
   c. give in to some demands to keep the peace.
   d. refuse to give in to any demands to keep the peace.

_____ 7. Hitler was able to annex Czechoslovakia and other nations because
   a. no one stopped him.
   b. the Czechs agreed with him.
   c. he defeated British guards.
   d. he defeated U.S. guards.

_____ 8. The West attempted to form an alliance with
   a. China.
   b. Japan.
   c. the Soviet Union.
   d. Turkey.

_____ 9. The German-Soviet nonaggression pact was an agreement to
   a. fight each other.
   b. defend each other.
   c. remain neutral.
   d. negotiate with each other.

_____ 10. Germany attempted to gain control of the Polish port of Danzig by
   a. negotiation.
   b. vote.
   c. attack.
   d. creating a protectorate.

Name _____ Class _____ Date _____

CHAPTER    Daily Quiz 30.3

Modern Chapter 21   **Axis Gains**

MATCHING *(10 points each)* In the space provided, write the letter of the term or place that matches each description. Some answers will not be used.

_____ 1. "lightning war"

_____ 2. people who help the enemy

_____ 3. French leader who surrendered to Hitler

_____ 4. French leader who formed the Free French government

_____ 5. French underground resistance fighters

_____ 6. German air force

_____ 7. German air attack on Britain

_____ 8. American law against participation in future wars

_____ 9. American act to supply Great Britain with war materials

_____ 10. statement of British and U.S. democratic goals

a. maquis
b. Charles de Gaulle
c. Atlantic Charter
d. Winston Churchill
e. Lend-Lease Act
f. blitzkrieg
g. Philippe Pétain
h. isolationists
i. Battle of Britain
j. collaborators
k. Neutrality Acts
l. Luftwaffe

Name _____ Class _____ Date _____

CHAPTER 30

Daily Quiz 30.4

Modern Chapter 21 — **The Soviet Union and the United States**

TRUE/FALSE Mark each statement *T* if it is true or *F* if it is false. If false explain why.

_____ 1. In 1940, Spain joined the Axis Powers.

_____ 2. The British were able to maintain control of Egypt and Greece after an attack led by Mussolini.

_____ 3. Axis advances into Africa, led by Erwin Rommel, hurt Allied forces.

_____ 4. Germany declared war on the Soviet Union after Soviets refused to renounce their claim to the Balkans.

_____ 5. At first, the Soviet appeal to the Allies for aid was ignored.

_____ 6. The Soviet scorched-earth policy, as well as the harsh winter, aided the Soviets in holding off Germany.

_____ 7. While aiding the Axis invasions, Japan halted its move into China.

_____ 8. The United States did not respond to Japan's actions in the Pacific.

_____ 9. Japan's attack on Pearl Harbor was the beginning of an attempt to take over the entire Pacific.

_____ 10. The United States helped the Philippines hold off Japan's invasion.

Name _____ Class _____ Date _____

Modern Chapter **21**

Daily Quiz 30.5

The Holocaust

MULTIPLE CHOICE *(10 points each)* For each of the following, write the letter of the best choice in the space provided.

_____ 1. Hitler's plan for a Europe with a single political and economic system was called the
   a. "New World."
   b. "New World Order."
   c. "New Order."
   d. "New Europe."

_____ 2. Hitler intended for the people of the Soviet Union to die out because the Slavs were
   a. racially inferior.
   b. enemies of Germany.
   c. potential spies.
   d. not hard workers.

_____ 3. Hitler's Final Solution was the
   a. extermination of the Slavs.
   b. extermination of the Jews.
   c. extermination of the Armenians.
   d. extermination of the British.

_____ 4. Heinrich Himmler headed the
   a. attack on Armenia.
   b. attack on the Soviet people.
   c. Final Solution.
   d. German secret police.

_____ 5. A systematic plan for concentration camps was outlined at the
   a. Potsdam Conference.
   b. Berlin Conference.
   c. Warsaw Conference.
   d. Wannsee Conference.

_____ 6. Auschwitz, Treblinka, Buchenwald, and Dachau were
   a. Jewish ghettos.
   b. concentration camps.
   c. German battlefields.
   d. German commanders.

_____ 7. Physically weak people in concentration camps were
   a. killed first.
   b. set free.
   c. used as servants.
   d. used as soldiers.

_____ 8. Hitler's Final Solution met with little resistance in eastern Europe because of
   a. secrecy.
   b. an anti-Semitic tradition.
   c. lack of living space.
   d. fear.

_____ 9. Jews were helped by, among others, the
   a. Danes.
   b. Turks.
   c. Poles.
   d. Finns.

_____ 10. The Swedish diplomat who helped Jews was
   a. Oskar Schindler.
   b. Raoul Wallenberg.
   c. Heinrich Himmler.
   d. Erwin Rommel.

Name _____ Class _____ Date _____

Daily Quiz 30.6

Modern Chapter 21

The End of the War

FILL IN THE BLANK *(10 points each)* For each of the following statements, fill in the blank with the appropriate word, phrase, or name.

1. The German army suffered a severe loss against the Soviets in the Battle of _____.

2. General Dwight D. Eisenhower and General Bernard Montgomery trapped Rommel's troops and retook _____ for the Allies.

3. Winston Churchill called Italy and the Balkans the _____, believing they could be attacked.

4. After Mussolini was forced to resign, the new premier, Marshal Pietro Badoglio, dissolved the _____.

5. American victory at Guadalcanal was important because it was Japanese territory, and it provided supplies to _____.

6. Island hopping means to attack some Japanese islands and _____.

7. _____ was the plan to retake France, beginning with a landing at Normandy.

8. V-E Day means _____.

9. At the meeting at _____, the Allies agreed to divide Germany between them.

10. Japan's surrender came after the _____.

Name _____ Class _____ Date _____

CHAPTER 31

Modern Chapter 22

Daily Quiz 31.1

Aftermath of the War in Europe

TRUE/FALSE Mark each statement *T* if it is true or *F* if it is false. If false explain why.

_____ 1. At the meeting in Yalta, the Allies decided that Eastern Europe would be put under military control.

_____ 2. Stalin believed that Eastern European nations should be taught socialist principles before they elected their own governments.

_____ 3. Churchill and Stalin proposed a United Nations organization to help maintain world security.

_____ 4. The Potsdam Conference set basic principles for postwar Germany, including its permanent division between East and West control.

_____ 5. The United States and Great Britain agreed that German industry needed to be completely dismantled to prevent swift German rearmament.

_____ 6. The Nürnberg trials deadlocked over whether to declare the Nazi Party a criminal organization.

_____ 7. The UN Security Council was open to any nation that wanted to join.

_____ 8. Italy and France voted to install dictatorships to restore stability.

_____ 9. The Soviets demanded that Eastern European nations install democracies along their borders to prevent fascist takeovers.

_____ 10. To achieve independence, Austria agreed to remain neutral.

Daily Quiz 31.2

Modern Chapter 22 — Origins of the Cold War

MULTIPLE CHOICE *(10 points each)* For each of the following, write the letter of the best choice in the space provided.

_____ 1. The Soviet Union and its supporters became known as
   a. Eastern bloc nations.
   b. European Communists.
   c. Soviet Pact nations.
   d. the Socialist Republics.

_____ 2. The Cold War can best be described as a
   a. war of ideas.
   b. war of attrition.
   c. guerilla war.
   d. war of technology.

_____ 3. The West believed that Stalin's "buffer nations" were a prelude to
   a. war.
   b. the expansion of fascism.
   c. the expansion of communism.
   d. economic disaster.

_____ 4. The Truman Doctrine stated that the United States would
   a. help prevent the spread of fascism.
   b. give war recovery money to Europe.
   c. become isolationist.
   d. help prevent the spread of communism.

_____ 5. The United States commitment to restrict the spread of communism was called
   a. isolationism.
   b. containment.
   c. Trumanism.
   d. anti-communism.

_____ 6. The Marshall Plan helped Europe recover
   a. militarily.
   b. politically.
   c. medically.
   d. economically.

_____ 7. The unsuccessful Soviet effort to appose the Marshall Plan was called
   a. the Stalin Plan.
   b. Cominform.
   c. Comintern.
   d. the Truman Doctrine.

_____ 8. The communist Yugoslavian government was expelled from the Cominform because it wanted
   a. independence.
   b. democracy.
   c. fascism.
   d. war reparations.

_____ 9. The distribution of food and materials to West Berlin was the
   a. Berlin blockade.
   b. Marshall Plan.
   c. UN Airlift.
   d. Berlin Airlift.

_____ 10. The mutual defense agreement among Eastern Bloc nations was known as
   a. the Cominform.
   b. the MDA.
   c. the Warsaw Pact.
   d. NATO.

Name _____ Class _____ Date _____

CHAPTER 31

Modern Chapter 22

Daily Quiz 31.3

Reconstruction, Reform, and Reaction in Europe

FILL IN THE BLANK *(10 points each)* For each of the following statements, fill in the blank with the appropriate word, phrase, or name.

1. West Germany's _____ economy helped its quick recovery from the war.

2. West German democracy was dominated by two parties, the Christian Democrats and _____.

3. The East German government put up the _____ to prevent their people from running to the West.

4. Britain's postwar socialist government created a _____ in which the government ran medical care and some industries.

5. France's Fourth Republic government fell because of the dispute over _____.

6. Charles de Gaulle's constitution for the Fifth Republic called for a strong _____.

7. The _____ stabilized tariffs, wages, and prices for its members.

8. _____ shocked Soviet leaders when he condemned Stalin and proposed social and economic reforms.

9. Eastern European nations attempted to solidify their economies with heavy industrialization and _____ farming.

10. Lack of freedom from the Soviet Union led to failed revolts in _____, _____ and _____.

Daily Quiz 31.4

Modern Chapter 22 — **The United States and Canada**

MATCHING *(10 points each)* In the space provided, write the letter of the term or place that matches each description. Some answers will not be used.

_____ 1. leader of anti-communist hysteria

_____ 2. created the Great Society program of reforms

_____ 3. civil rights organization

_____ 4. desegregated schools

_____ 5. civil rights activist

_____ 6. attempt to stop communist advances in South Korea

_____ 7. provision for economic and military anticommunist assistance in Middle East

_____ 8. president who oversaw the Cuban missile crisis

_____ 9. U.S. and Soviet standoff over communist armament

_____ 10. separatist Canadian organization

a. Joseph McCarthy
b. Southeast Asia Treaty Organization
c. *Brown v. Board of Education of Topeka*
d. Eisenhower Doctrine
e. Lyndon Johnson
f. NAACP
g. Cuban missile crisis
h. John F. Kennedy
i. Martin Luther King, Jr.
j. Fidel Castro
k. DEW Line
l. Parti Quebecois

Name _____ Class _____ Date _____

Modern Chapter 23

Daily Quiz 32.1

South Asia After Empire

MULTIPLE CHOICE *(10 points each)* For each of the following, write the letter of the best choice in the space provided.

_____ 1. Britain did not have the support of India during World War II because
   a. of a neutrality pact.
   b. India demanded self-rule.
   c. of German occupation.
   d. of Japanese occupation.

_____ 2. Muhammad Ali Jinnah led the Indian movement for
   a. Indian independence.
   b. Palestinian independence.
   c. a separate Hindu state.
   d. a separate Muslim state.

_____ 3. The partitioning of India was further complicated by demands of
   a. British Indian citizens.
   b. the Buddhist minority.
   c. the Sikh minority.
   d. the Shi'ah minority.

_____ 4. India's first prime minister was
   a. Mohandas Gandhi.
   b. Indira Gandhi.
   c. Jawaharlal Nehru.
   d. Muhammad Ali Jinnah.

_____ 5. Nehru's policy against alliance with the U.S. or U.S.S.R. was called
   a. nonalignment.
   b. nonagreement.
   c. separatism.
   d. the resistance.

_____ 6. A combination of nationalized and private industry is called a
   a. command economy.
   b. market economy.
   c. partial economy.
   d. mixed economy.

_____ 7. Relations between India and China were complicated by
   a. the occupation of Tibet.
   b. the occupation of Pakistan.
   c. Chinese Sikh immigration.
   d. Chinese Hindu immigration.

_____ 8. India and Pakistan divided over the nationality of
   a. Kashmir.
   b. Punjab.
   c. Tibet.
   d. Nepal.

_____ 9. Geographical separation and political differences led to the creation of Bangladesh, formerly
   a. East Pakistan.
   b. West Pakistan.
   c. Kashmir.
   d. Punjab.

_____ 10. The first woman to head a Muslim state was
   a. Indira Gandhi.
   b. Ali Bhutto.
   c. Benazir Bhutto.
   d. Dalai Lama.

Name _____ Class _____ Date _____

Daily Quiz 32.2

Modern Chapter 23 **Communist China and Its Influence**

TRUE/FALSE Mark each statement *T* if it is true or *F* if it is false. If false explain why.

_____ 1. Chinese Nationalists and Chinese Communists joined together to fight Japan.

_____ 2. After the war, Chiang Kai-shek formed the People's Republic of China.

_____ 3. The Great Leap Forward, based on a push to increase industry, helped balance production of material and consumer goods.

_____ 4. Mao Zedong's Cultural Revolution aimed to destroy China's culture and history.

_____ 5. Jiang Qing's Gang of Four fought moderates to continue the Cultural Revolution.

_____ 6. Under Deng Xiaoping, the economy improved, but China remained closed to the West.

_____ 7. The Tiananmen Square Massacre was caused by a call for a return to hard-line Communism.

_____ 8. During the Cold War, China supported communist North Korea against U.S. troops and republican South Korea.

_____ 9. Both South Korea's and North Korea's economies suffered after the war.

_____ 10. China regards Taiwan as an independent nation.

Name _____ Class _____ Date _____

CHAPTER 32

Modern Chapter 23

Daily Quiz 32.3

The Japanese Miracle

FILL IN THE BLANK *(10 points each)* For each of the following statements, fill in the blank with the appropriate word, phrase, or name.

1. MacArthur's first step in the occupation of Japan was to _____ the country.

2. The "MacArthur Constitution" called for a _____ with direct elections.

3. The constitution also stated that _____ was not a natural right of Japan.

4. Japanese economic reforms included the breakup of the _____, or powerful family-owned firms.

5. The economic success that began in the 1960s was rooted in Japan's new focus on _____.

6. Economic success led to a higher standard in living, but a decline in the traditional emphasis on the _____.

7. Despite events in China and North Korea, and U.S. encouragement, Japan resisted a return to _____.

8. Japan's move toward independence and the postwar U.S. _____ presence caused tension between the two countries.

9. Japan attempted to warm relations with Russia, but they were not able to resolve the issue of the _____.

10. The primary political party in Japan is the _____.

Name _____ Class _____ Date _____

Daily Quiz 32.4

Modern Chapter 23   **Independence Struggles in Southeast Asia**

MATCHING *(10 points each)* In the space provided, write the letter of the term or place that matches each description. Some answers will not be used.

_____ 1. leader of the party that opposed Marcos, assassinated in 1983

_____ 2. leader of the Philippines who restored democracy

_____ 3. leader against French occupation who brought communism to North Vietnam

_____ 4. belief that the fall of South Vietnam to communism would lead to the fall of rest of Southeast Asia

_____ 5. major attack by North Vietnam

_____ 6. removed U.S. forces from Vietnam and led to Vietnam's reunification

_____ 7. Vietnamese refugees

_____ 8. supply line in Laos, connecting North and South Vietnam

_____ 9. Cambodian communist group

_____ 10. brutal Khmer Rouge leader

a. Paris Peace Accords
b. Ho Chi Minh
c. Tet Offensive
d. Benigno Aquino
e. Corazon Aquino
f. domino theory
g. Aung San Suu Kyi
h. Ho Chi Minh Trail
i. Geneva Accord
j. Pol Pot
k. Khmer Rouge
l. "boat people"

Name _____ Class _____ Date _____

Modern Chapter 23

Daily Quiz 32.5
Asian Paths to Prosperity

MULTIPLE CHOICE *(10 points each)* For each of the following, write the letter of the best choice in the space provided.

_____ 1. One reason why authoritarian control became common in Asia is because of
   a. ethnic conflict.
   b. little Western influence.
   c. distrust of Western ideas.
   d. good economies.

_____ 2. Many Asian countries believed that the economy grew faster with
   a. a market economy.
   b. government control.
   c. Western investors.
   d. a strong democracy.

_____ 3. An example of a economically successful, tightly controlled country is
   a. Burma.
   b. Singapore.
   c. Thailand.
   d. Laos.

_____ 4. Many Asian countries had difficulty establishing postcolonial economies because they had
   a. little of their own wealth.
   b. trade ties to an empire.
   c. communist beliefs.
   d. religious conflicts.

_____ 5. Asia's heavy dependence on foreign investment has led to
   a. economic crises.
   b. financial success.
   c. weak government.
   d. increased tourism.

_____ 6. ASEAN is
   a. an economic cooperation group.
   b. a mutual defense group.
   c. a disarmament pact.
   d. a cooperative navy.

_____ 7. Attempts to strengthen economies sometimes led to
   a. an increase in labor unions.
   b. a decrease in labor unions.
   c. more workers' rights.
   d. the lack of labor force.

_____ 8. South Korea, Taiwan, Singapore, and Hong Kong were known as the "Four Tigers" because of
   a. military strength.
   b. economic strength.
   c. agricultural weakness.
   d. their tourist economies.

_____ 9. The popularity of Asian-produced goods created
   a. competition for the West.
   b. an economic bubble.
   c. weak currency.
   d. trade cooperation.

_____ 10. Japanese success has led Westen businesses to
   a. place heavy tariffs on Japanese imports.
   b. sabotage Japanese marketing.
   c. copy Japanese methods.
   d. dispute trade agreements.

Name _____ Class _____ Date _____

Daily Quiz 33.1

Modern Chapter 24   African Independence After World War II

MATCHING *(10 points each)* In the space provided, write the letter of the term or place that matches each description. Some answers will not be used.

_____ 1. movement for cultural unity and freedom in Africa

_____ 2. leader of CPP and believer in Gold Coast independence

_____ 3. Kikuyu leader who united Kenya and led independence drive

_____ 4. Kikuyu terrorist organization

_____ 5. postwar group of colonies, with some political rights for natives

_____ 6. rejected French aid to achieve independence for Guinea

_____ 7. Congolese dictator

_____ 8. government segregation of races

_____ 9. antiapartheid leader and first African president of South Africa

_____ 10. South African city where schoolchildren protesting were attacked by police

a. French Union
b. Pan-Africanism
c. Jomo Kenyatta
d. Nelson Mandela
e. Mau Mau
f. Soweto
g. apartheid
h. Kwame Nkrumah
i. Sékou Touré
j. Sierra Leone
k. Joseph Mobutu
l. African National Congress

Name _____ Class _____ Date _____

CHAPTER 33

Modern Chapter 24

Daily Quiz 33.2

Africa Since Independence

TRUE/FALSE Mark each statement *T* if it is true or *F* if it is false. If false explain why.

_____ 1. The economy of Ghana kept Kwame Nkrumah from gaining absolute power.

_____ 2. Ghana's economy improved under Jerry Rawlings' rule, but the people of Ghana still sought civilian rule.

_____ 3. Ethnic fighting caused Biafra to split from Nigeria and permanently establish independence.

_____ 4. Religious differences tore Rwanda and Burundi apart.

_____ 5. Zaire helped the Tutsi refugees expel the Hutu.

_____ 6. The Tutsi gained power when rebels against Zaire's leadership joined their fight.

_____ 7. Many African nations thrived on their success with single, easily exported products.

_____ 8. The end of the Cold War caused tensions in Angola to worsen.

_____ 9. The United Nations successfully intervened in Somalia after power struggles between clans broke out.

_____ 10. In the postcolonial era, Africa has helped to support a renewed interest in its history and culture.

Name _____ Class _____ Date _____

Modern Chapter 24

Daily Quiz 33.3

Nationalism in the Middle East and North Africa

FILL IN THE BLANK *(10 points each)* For each of the following statements, fill in the blank with the appropriate word, phrase, or name.

1. In postwar Algeria, most of the power was held by a community of Europeans called _____.

2. In 1962, Charles de Gaulle surprised many French when he _____.

3. In 1939, Britain reversed the Balfour Declaration and began to support the creation of an _____ in Palestine.

4. After Britain withdrew from Palestine, the UN divided it into _____.

5. The UN's plan led to war, won by _____, creating tension among the rest of the Arab nations.

6. To resolve the _____, the United States sided against Britain, leading to the final withdrawal of Europe from Egypt.

7. Ba'athist governments in the Middle East adopted socialism, but those governments drifted toward _____.

8. The growing strength of _____ led Syria to break away from the United Arab Republic.

9. Fear of Soviet influence led the United States to place Mohammad Reza Pahlavi as leader of _____.

10. After the execution of Adnan Menderes, Turkey returned to _____ rule and the reforms of Kemal and Inönü.

Name _____ Class _____ Date _____

CHAPTER 33

Modern Chapter 24

Daily Quiz 33.4

War, Revolution, and Oil in the Middle East and North Africa

MULTIPLE CHOICE *(10 points each)* For each of the following, write the letter of the best choice in the space provided.

_____ 1. During the Six-Day War, Egyptian, Syrian, and Jordanian territory was captured by
   a. Palestine.
   b. Iraq.
   c. Israel.
   d. the UN.

_____ 2. Displaced Palestinians felt their best hope lay with
   a. the UN.
   b. the United States.
   c. Egypt.
   d. the PLO.

_____ 3. Egypt and Syria planned a secret attack on Israel during the time that the Israeli prime minister was
   a. Golda Meir.
   b. Yasir Arafat.
   c. Shimon Peres.
   d. Gamal Abdel Nasser.

_____ 4. Anwar Sadat and Menachem Begin met in the United States and signed a peace framework known as the
   a. Camp David Accords.
   b. Camp David Treaty.
   c. Sadat-Begin Agreement.
   d. Egypt-Israel Peace.

_____ 5. Israeli-occupied territories led to a Palestinian intifada, or
   a. peace treaty.
   b. disarmament.
   c. intelligence operation.
   d. uprising.

_____ 6. Israeli Prime Minister Yitzhak Rabin's attempts at peace treaties between Israel and Palestine led to
   a. a Palestinian state.
   b. Palestinian self-rule.
   c. the end of the PLO.
   d. Rabin's assassination.

_____ 7. Oil-producing nations increased their bargaining power by
   a. forming OPEC.
   b. eliminating other power sources.
   c. taking over other oil-producing areas.
   d. signing peace treaties.

_____ 8. The overthrow of the Shah of Iran was prompted by
   a. desire for modernization.
   b. fear of Western influence.
   c. Shi'ah prejudice.
   d. government corruption.

_____ 9. Iraq's invasion of Kuwait was based on an attempt to
   a. put down the Kurd minority.
   b. move against Iran.
   c. gain control of more oil.
   d. attack Saudi Arabia.

_____ 10. The coalition success of Operation Desert Storm led to
   a. the fall of Hussein's government.
   b. Iraqi democracy.
   c. Kurdish independence.
   d. economic sanctions.

Name _____ Class _____ Date _____

Daily Quiz 34.1

Modern Chapter 25

Facing New Challenges

TRUE/FALSE Mark each statement *T* if it is true or *F* if it is false. If false explain why.

_____ 1. Profits from multinational corporations helped to speed industrialization of Latin American countries.

_____ 2. Monoculture refers to a movement to bring back traditional Latin American folk culture.

_____ 3. Reliance on exports of only one or two crops led to economic instability in Latin American countries.

_____ 4. Debts from foreign loans and domestic expenses caused inflation in the 1980s.

_____ 5. The Andean Pact was a mutual defense agreement.

_____ 6. Mexico was hurt by the trade restrictions of the North American Free Trade Agreement.

_____ 7. During the shift to industrialization, Latin America's population suddenly dropped.

_____ 8. Many Latin Americans moved to the United States to find jobs.

_____ 9. Mothers of the Plaza de Mayo is an Argentinian political party.

_____ 10. The Organization of American States is part of a plan to create a unified, single currency in Latin America.

Name _____ Class _____ Date _____

Modern Chapter 25

Daily Quiz 34.2
Mexico and Central America

MATCHING *(10 points each)* In the space provided, write the letter of the term or place that matches each description. Some answers will not be used.

_____ 1. postwar, anti-reform Mexican political party

_____ 2. president who encouraged free trade and investment

_____ 3. Marxist Nicaraguan rebel group

_____ 4. Sandinista Nicaraguan leader

_____ 5. Nicaraguan leader who became president after winning a free election

_____ 6. Salvadoran left-wing guerrilla group

_____ 7. U.S.-funded Nicaraguan guerrilla group

_____ 8. Panamanian dictator jailed for drug trafficking

_____ 9. plan promoting negotiations instead of violence

_____ 10. promoted peace for Central America

a. Manuel Noriega
b. Violeta Barrios de Chamorro
c. PRI
d. Daniel Ortega
e. PEMEX
f. junta
g. contras
h. Carlos Salinas de Gortari
i. Contadora Principles
j. Oscar Arias
k. Sandinistas
l. FMLN

Name _____ Class _____ Date _____

Daily Quiz 34.3

Modern Chapter 25

Nations of the Caribbean

MULTIPLE CHOICE *(10 points each)* For each of the following, write the letter of the best choice in the space provided.

_____ 1. Fidel Castro overthrew the government of
   a. Daniel Ortega.
   b. Manuel Noriega.
   c. Fulgencio Batista.
   d. Oscar Arias.

_____ 2. Cubans agreed with Castro's vision of a Cuba free from
   a. Spanish rule.
   b. Soviet influence.
   c. American influence.
   d. Asian influence.

_____ 3. Castro's government could best be described as a
   a. dictatorship.
   b. democracy.
   c. diplomacy.
   d. monarchy.

_____ 4. Castro's rule had a positive impact on
   a. trade.
   b. international relations.
   c. education.
   d. transportation systems.

_____ 5. One reason the U.S. thought the Bay of Pigs invasion would be successful was because
   a. of Castro's surrender.
   b. Castro signed a peace treaty.
   c. of expected Cuban anti-Castro support.
   d. of British military backing.

_____ 6. Cuba's economy was affected by
   a. natural disasters.
   b. a small labor force.
   c. U.S.-led boycotts.
   d. poor investments.

_____ 7. By 1952, Puerto Rico had moved from being a territory to
   a. a commonwealth.
   b. a protectorate.
   c. a state.
   d. independence.

_____ 8. Operation Bootstrap was
   a. a healthcare program.
   b. an economic program.
   c. a failed Cuban invasion.
   d. a failed bid for statehood.

_____ 9. Jean-Bertrand Aristide's presidency in Haiti was different because he
   a. was a dictator.
   b. was a priest.
   c. opened up the economy.
   d. completed his term peacefully.

_____ 10. The United States invaded Grenada to
   a. put down a socialist rebellion.
   b. put down a communist rebellion.
   c. destroy Soviet missiles.
   d. fight Cuba.

Name _____ Class _____ Date _____

CHAPTER 34

Modern Chapter 25

Daily Quiz 34.4

South America

FILL IN THE BLANK *(10 points each)* For each of the following statements, fill in the blank with the appropriate word, phrase, or name.

1. Brazil's military government seemed to improve the economy, but the nation actually had the highest _____ in the world.

2. Juan Perón rose to power in Argentina because of the support of the _____.

3. Perón's power and support was largely due to the popularity of _____.

4. Desaparecidos, or _____, were part of the Argentine military's "dirty war."

5. The Argentine military tried, but failed, to gain the _____.

6. _____ was a Peruvian guerrilla group who operated with Maoist beliefs.

7. Both the MRTA and Shining Path financed their actions from the _____ business.

8. Colombia's participation in the _____ brought crime and violence to its cities.

9. The Colombian authorities asked the _____ to intervene and help capture drug traffickers.

10. Under Augusto Pinochet, Chile's economy prospered, but he was later arrested for abuses of _____.

Name _____ Class _____ Date _____

Daily Quiz 35.1

Modern Chapter 26 — The Industrial Powers of North America

MATCHING *(10 points each)* In the space provided, write the letter of the term or place that matches each description. Some answers will not be used.

_____ 1. president who resigned before being impeached

_____ 2. Nixon's plan for U.S. troop withdrawal

_____ 3. scandal that began with break-in of the Democratic National Committee

_____ 4. president whose optimistic outlook helped him win reelection

_____ 5. scandal based on illegal arms sales and support of Nicaraguan rebels

_____ 6. president who was impeached, but did not resign

_____ 7. combination of decreased economic activity, high unemployment, and high prices

_____ 8. planned power outages to conserve energy

_____ 9. statement that United States would regard attempts to control Persian Gulf as assault on U.S. interests

_____ 10. statement that said Quebec was a distinct society

a. Iran-contra affair
b. Carter Doctrine
c. Bill Clinton
d. Watergate
e. Richard Nixon
f. "rolling blackouts"
g. Vietnamization
h. Ronald Reagan
i. stagflation
j. Pierre Trudeau
k. Meech Lake Accord
l. Jimmy Carter

Name _____ Class _____ Date _____

Daily Quiz 35.2

Modern Chapter 26

Europe

MULTIPLE CHOICE *(10 points each)* For each of the following, write the letter of the best choice in the space provided.

_____ 1. Thatcherism was based on
   a. reduction of social programs.
   b. increase of social programs.
   c. nationalization of industries.
   d. increased defense spending.

_____ 2. Northern Ireland's Catholics resented the state's
   a. lack of representation.
   b. Protestant domination.
   c. trade restrictions.
   d. poll tax.

_____ 3. The goal of the IRA is
   a. a united Ireland.
   b. a Catholic British state.
   c. a free Northern Ireland.
   d. removal of British military.

_____ 4. Under François Mitterand, the government became
   a. weaker.
   b. stronger.
   c. communist.
   d. militaristic.

_____ 5. Willy Brandt instituted a policy called Ostpolitik, meant to
   a. improve relations with Eastern Europe.
   b. isolate Germany.
   c. absorb East Germany.
   d. remove democracy.

_____ 6. One of Germany's biggest problems after reunification was
   a. East Germany's secret police.
   b. West Germany's immigration fears.
   c. East Germany's weak economy.
   d. West Germany's weak economy.

_____ 7. After the death of Francisco Franco, Juan Carlos
   a. restored communism.
   b. rejoined NATO.
   c. restored democracy.
   d. restored a strong monarchy.

_____ 8. Spain faced terrorists from the ETA, who were
   a. communist guerrillas.
   b. an Irish Catholic group.
   c. Yugoslavian separatists.
   d. a Basque separatist group.

_____ 9. The Helsinki Accords established guidelines for human rights and
   a. defense agreements.
   b. trade routes.
   c. settling boundary disputes.
   d. settling immigration disputes.

_____ 10. The European Union planned to create a Europe with
   a. a common currency.
   b. a common government.
   c. isolationist tendencies.
   d. no borders.

Daily Quiz 35.3

The Fall of Communism

FILL IN THE BLANK *(10 points each)* For each of the following statements, fill in the blank with the appropriate word, phrase, or name.

1. The Brezhnev Doctrine stated that the Soviet Union would intervene if any satellite nation _____.

2. Although the Soviet Union was supposed to be moving toward peace, the 1979 invasion of _____ weakened relations with the West.

3. Gorbachev's policies of _____ and _____ were meant to open up and restructure the Soviet Union.

4. After the breakup of the Soviet Union, _____ became president of the largest state, the Federation of Russia.

5. After the fall of communism, Russia fell victim to a wave of _____, including drug trafficking and black market goods.

6. One of new Russia's biggest problems was a brutal fight to retain control of _____, a Muslim region valued for its oil.

7. Lech Walesa led the fight to end communism in _____.

8. The "Velvet Revolution" refers to the smooth transition to democracy in _____.

9. The breakup of Yugoslavia was difficult because of the many different ethnicities and _____ in the regions.

10. The _____ gave Bosnian Serbs control over specific regions while still recognizing the overall sovereignty of Bosnia's Muslim-led government.

Name _____ Class _____ Date _____

CHAPTER 35

Modern Chapter 26

Daily Quiz 35.4

A Day That Changed the World

TRUE/FALSE Mark each statement *T* if it is true or *F* if it is false. If false explain why.

_____ 1. Both of the World Trade Center towers were completely destroyed in a terrorist attack using hijacked commercial jetliners.

_____ 2. The assault on New York City constituted the extent of the terrorist attack.

_____ 3. There were not enough medical personnel to deal with the flood of injured people pulled from the wreckage of the World Trade Center.

_____ 4. The investigation involved cooperation between the United States and other nations.

_____ 5. Islamic extremists, some of whom had lived and trained as pilots in the United States, were suspected of carrying out the September 11 attacks.

_____ 6. The Bush administration launched a war on terrorism, and an offensive was begun against an Islamic terrorist group based in Afghanistan that was blamed for the attacks.

_____ 7. The federal government was unable to offer financial assistance to the recovery effort.

_____ 8. Several thousand New York City firefighters were killed on the day of the attacks.

_____ 9. The people of the United States put aside their political differences and rallied to assist the recovery through donations of blood and funds for relief.

_____ 10. The Taliban government, which has supported the al Qaeda terrorist group, was forced from power in Afghanistan by U.S. and allied forces.

Name _____ Class _____ Date _____

Modern Chapter 27

Daily Quiz 36.1

The Arts and Literature

MATCHING *(10 points each)* In the space provided, write the letter of the term or place that matches each description. Some answers will not be used.

_____ 1. used art as an expression of the unconscious mind

_____ 2. style featuring elements of everyday life and culture

_____ 3. style featuring shapes and colors to create illusions

_____ 4. where the artist is a living work of art

_____ 5. designed buildings influenced by machinery

_____ 6. groundbreaking musical group of the 1960s

_____ 7. movement that promoted the *auteur* theory

_____ 8. political playwright who focused on the artificiality of theatrical experience

_____ 9. a group of writers who criticized materialism and commercialism in American life

_____ 10. Arab writer attacked for his treatment of Islam

a. Beats
b. performance art
c. pop art
d. op art
e. Martha Graham
f. Jackson Pollack
g. conceptual art
h. Le Corbusier
i. "New Wave"
j. Naguib Mahfouz
k. Maya Angelou
l. Bertolt Brecht
m. the Beatles

Name _____ Class _____ Date _____

Modern Chapter 27

Daily Quiz 36.2
Science and Technology

MULTIPLE CHOICE *(10 points each)* For each of the following, write the letter of the best choice in the space provided.

_____ 1. In 1957, Yury Gagarin became the first person to
  a. break the sound barrier.
  b. land on the moon.
  c. build a satellite.
  d. orbit Earth.

_____ 2. In 1998, the United States, Russia, and fourteen other nations began to build
  a. an unmanned spacecraft.
  b. a manned space station.
  c. a space shuttle.
  d. an Earth shield.

_____ 3. The transistor is an example of
  a. computerization.
  b. nuclear technology.
  c. miniaturization.
  d. high speed technology.

_____ 4. Charles Babbage's "analytical machine" was an early
  a. silicon chip.
  b. computer.
  c. synthesizer.
  d. robot.

_____ 5. E-commerce refers to
  a. the sale of computers.
  b. business on the Internet.
  c. electronic mail.
  d. software downloads.

_____ 6. The intense beams of light that have become part of medical and communication technology are
  a. microchips.
  b. silicon chips.
  c. radars.
  d. lasers.

_____ 7. The "wonder drugs" that kill bacteria and fight diseases are
  a. vaccines.
  b. epidemics.
  c. antibiotics.
  d. bacterias.

_____ 8. The genetic code is a map that interprets the
  a. activity of the brain.
  b. structure of DNA.
  c. structure of bacteria.
  d. way vaccines work.

_____ 9. The variety of animals and plants that naturally occur in an environment is known as
  a. biodiversity.
  b. urbanization.
  c. forestation.
  d. flora and fauna.

_____ 10. An increase in gases in the Earth's atmosphere can lead to
  a. ozone thinning.
  b. global warming.
  c. chemicals.
  d. an Ice Age.

Daily Quiz 36.3

Modern Chapter 27

Human Rights and the Spread of Democratic Ideals

FILL IN THE BLANK *(10 points each)* For each of the following statements, fill in the blank with the appropriate word, phrase, or name.

1. The Universal Declaration of Human Rights was adopted by the _____.

2. The declaration was marred by some nations' arguments that attempts to enforce the declaration would violate their _____.

3. Ethnic cleansing, terrorist acts, and imprisonment or execution for speaking against a government are examples of _____.

4. _____ is a private organization that investigates and reports human rights abuses.

5. Nations may differ on their view of human rights; for example, some countries value _____ more than the rights of the individual.

6. Some argue that the best way to fight abuses of rights in extremely poor countries is to improve their _____.

7. The fall of communism means that many _____ and authoritarian regimes have also lost hold.

8. Although China has moved towards a free market economy, the government has prevented _____ movements.

9. Even though it no longer has the support of the _____, Cuba is still under the communist rule of Castro.

10. The military government in _____ prevented Aung San Suu Kyi from receiving her Nobel Peace Prize in person.

Name _____ Class _____ Date _____

EPILOGUE

Daily Quiz E.1
Revolution to Imperialism

MULTIPLE CHOICE *(10 points each)* For each of the following, write the letter of the best choice in the space provided.

_____ 1. Louis XIV of France believed in
   a. creating a republic.
   b. the divine right of kings.
   c. a feudalist monarchy.
   d. isolating France.

_____ 2. Oliver Cromwell deposed Charles I and made England into a
   a. Scottish colony.
   b. commonwealth.
   c. small group of city-states.
   d. theocracy.

_____ 3. The English Bill of Rights established the power of the
   a. Parliament over the ruler.
   b. people over the ruler.
   c. ruler over Parliament.
   d. Anglican Church.

_____ 4. Enlightenment thinkers believed in
   a. simple religion.
   b. absolute monarchy.
   c. spiritual answers.
   d. reason and science.

_____ 5. The French Revolution tried to
   a. fight religious freedom.
   b. promote free trade.
   c. give the people a voice.
   d. empower another emperor.

_____ 6. Napoléon's rule did not represent the ideal of the Revolution because he
   a. was essentially a dictator.
   b. was really a mercantilist.
   c. believed in expansion.
   d. had a state religion.

_____ 7. The Congress of Vienna led to the weakening of France by surrounding it with
   a. a ring of strong states.
   b. armed revolutionaries.
   c. several monarchs.
   d. hundreds of delegates.

_____ 8. Capitalism, socialism, and communism all dealt with
   a. ways of doing business.
   b. economic theory.
   c. scientific method.
   d. absolute monarchies.

_____ 9. The rebellion of colonies and unification of states grew out of a sense of
   a. empiricism.
   b. socialism.
   c. nationalism.
   d. statism.

_____ 10. The attempt of a powerful nation to dominate another is
   a. nationalism.
   b. empiricism.
   c. communism.
   d. imperialism.

EPILOGUE

Daily Quiz E.2
World War in the Twentieth Century

TRUE/FALSE Mark each statement *T* if it is true or *F* if it is false. If false explain why.

_____ 1. Growing empires avoided forming alliances in order to defend themselves better.

_____ 2. Serbian anger over Austria-Hungary's annexation of Bosnia and Herzegovina led to the beginnings of World War II.

_____ 3. World War I was especially deadly because of new weapons.

_____ 4. Religious disputes led to the Russian Revolution.

_____ 5. The Treaty of Versailles realigned Europe and punished Serbia by lessening its powers.

_____ 6. World War I economically weakened the United States and Europe.

_____ 7. Economically weakened European countries allowed radical leaders to come to power.

_____ 8. As the European empires divided and weakened, colonies began to fight for their independence.

_____ 9. Asian countries blamed a lack of Westernization for their economic problems.

_____ 10. Aggressive attempts to increase territory by Allied powers led to World War II.

EPILOGUE

Daily Quiz E.3
Europe and the Americas since 1945

MATCHING *(10 points each)* In the space provided, write the letter of the term or place that matches each description. Some answers will not be used.

_____ 1. United States pledge of support to nations resisting communism

_____ 2. Policy lifting trade barriers between United States, Mexico, and Canada

_____ 3. United States program to assist European nations in rebuilding their economies

_____ 4. International organization formed to maintain world peace and cooperation

_____ 5. economy where all decisions are made by government

_____ 6. Standoff between United States and Soviet Union over Soviet armament of Cuba

_____ 7. policy to restrict the spread of communism

_____ 8. Ideological battle between Western governments and the communist Soviet Union

_____ 9. American civil rights leader

_____ 10. Mutual defense agreement between European communist nations

a. command economy
b. containment
c. Nürnberg, Germany
d. Cold War
e. Martin Luther King, Jr.
f. Cuban missile crisis
g. Yalta and Potsdam
h. Truman Doctrine
i. Marshall Plan
j. Warsaw Pact
k. United Nations
l. North American Free Trade Agreement

Name _____ Class _____ Date _____

EPILOGUE   Daily Quiz E.4
Asia, Africa, and the Middle East Since 1945

FILL IN THE BLANK *(10 points each)* For each of the following statements, fill in the blank with the appropriate word, phrase, or name.

1. Japan's economic strength after the 1960s depended on _____ to the United States.

2. China's _____ resulted in a destructive decrease of production and food shortages.

3. Mao Zedong's _____ was an attempt to violently enforce social change.

4. Corazon Aquino brought constitutional democracy and free enterprise back to _____.

5. _____ was led to communist rule by Ho Chi Minh.

6. After winning independence from Britain, Muslims in India formed the state of _____, while the rest of India remained Hindu.

7. _____ became the first woman to head a Muslim nation, Bangladesh.

8. Nelson Mandela fought to eliminate the policy of _____ in South Africa.

9. Fighting broke out in the Middle East after _____ was divided into Jewish and Arab states.

10. The _____ were one attempt to form a peace agreement between Israel and Palestine.

Name _____ Class _____ Date _____

(EPILOGUE)

Daily Quiz E.5
The Modern Era and Beyond

MATCHING *(10 points each)* In the space provided, write the letter of the term or place that matches each description. Some answers will not be used.

_____ 1. Soviet leader who introduced reforms which ended communism

_____ 2. First president of Russia in the post-Soviet world

_____ 3. United States president known for optimistic view of America

_____ 4. European nations joined by free trade and common currency

_____ 5. Openness, part of Soviet reforms

_____ 6. Restructuring, part of Soviet reforms

_____ 7. ability to create smaller, lighter materials

_____ 8. Separatist French-speaking Canadian province

_____ 9. United States president impeached by House of Representatives

_____ 10. First person to walk on the moon

a. European Union
b. perestroika
c. miniaturization
d. Boris Yeltsin
e. Bill Clinton
f. Maastricht Treaty
g. Quebec
h. Neil Armstrong
i. Ronald Reagan
j. glasnost
k. Mikhail Gorbachev
l. Chechnya

Name _____ Class _____ Date _____

EPILOGUE

Daily Quiz E.6

A Day That Changed the World

TRUE/FALSE Mark each statement *T* if it is true or *F* if it is false. If false explain why.

_____ 1. Both of the World Trade Center towers were completely destroyed in a terrorist attack using hijacked commercial jetliners.

_____ 2. The assault on New York City constituted the extent of the terrorist attack.

_____ 3. There were insufficient medical personnel to deal with the flood of injured people immediately following the terrorist attacks.

_____ 4. The attacks led to increased unity between the United States and many foreign nations.

_____ 5. The attacks were carried out by Islamic extremists who had lived in the United States.

_____ 6. The United States declared a war on terrorism, and an offensive was begun against an Islamic terrorist group, based in Afghanistan, that was blamed for the attacks.

_____ 7. The impact of the attacks on the economy was extreme, and efforts to revive the economy largely failed.

_____ 8. Roughly 6,000 people were killed on the day of the attacks.

_____ 9. The people of the United States could not get past their ideological differences to find the psychological stability necessary to allow them to cope with the attacks.

_____ 10. Osama bin Laden, the head of the al Qaeda terrorist group, was blamed for the attacks against the United States.

Name _____ Class _____ Date _____

PROLOGUE

Daily Quiz P.1

The First Civilizations

FILL IN THE BLANK *(10 Points each)* Complete the statements below by filling in the blanks.

1. Land bridges that formed during the _____ helped human life spread throughout the world.

2. During the _____, some peoples began to settle in villages and to develop permanent ways of life.

3. Government, food production, and a _____ are characteristics of civilization.

4. People settled in the valley near the _____ because yearly floods created a rich soil that was good for farming.

5. Egyptians used _____ to redraw boundaries of fields after floods and also to build the pyramids.

6. _____ encouraged the belief in a monotheistic religion in Egypt.

7. _____ are made up of cities and the lands, fields, and villages nearby.

8. Most of the upper Tigris-Euphrates valley was eventually conquered by _____.

9. Phoenician city-states were governed by _____.

10. The laws of the Hebrew people appear in the _____.

Name _____ Class _____ Date _____

PROLOGUE

Daily Quiz P.2
Ancient India and China

TRUE/FALSE *(10 points each)* Mark each statement *T* if it is true or *F* if it is false. If false explain why.

_____ 1. In the Indo-Aryan social system, merchants were the most important people.

_____ 2. Hindus view karma as a negative force as well as a positive force.

_____ 3. Right views, or seeing life as it truly is, is one of the Four Noble Truths.

_____ 4. Buddhism differed from Hinduism because Buddhists did not accept Hindu gods.

_____ 5. Chinese civilization was greatly impacted by traders from Indo-European civilizations.

_____ 6. China's first dynasty developed along the Huang River.

_____ 7. The Shang dynasty developed religious beliefs such as animism, the worship of ancestors.

_____ 8. The Qin dynasty ended when the royal line died out.

_____ 9. Daoism asks people to study and follow the ways of nature.

_____ 10. The Han dynasty, which followed both Legalist and Confucian ideas, was harsher than the Qin.

Name _____ Class _____ Date _____

PROLOGUE

Daily Quiz P.3
Civilizations of the Mediterranean World

MULTIPLE CHOICE *(10 points each)* For each of the following, write the letter of the best choice in the space provided.

_____ 1. Many Greek city-states were built around an acropolis, or
  a. emperor.
  b. public meeting place.
  c. hilltop.
  d. coastline.

_____ 2. Greek religion tried to explain the natural world and
  a. human actions.
  b. moral issues.
  c. ethical monotheism.
  d. the *Iliad*.

_____ 3. Sparta waged a battle against Athens in the
  a. Hellenistic Wars.
  b. Peloponnesian War.
  c. Homeric War.
  d. Cleisthenes War.

_____ 4. Greek thinkers tried to explain natural events through
  a. athletic strength.
  b. moral choices.
  c. fate and destiny.
  d. logical reasoning.

_____ 5. Alexander's empire fell because when he died
  a. the Persians and Greeks could not work together.
  b. his family left the empire.
  c. his generals divided the empire.
  d. poor people revolted.

_____ 6. The Roman Republic ended because of
  a. democratic rule.
  b. too much expansion.
  c. Julius Caesar's dictatorship.
  d. the people's revolt.

_____ 7. Augustus Caesar's rule began the
  a. Roman Empire.
  b. Imperial Empire.
  c. Western Empire.
  d. Augustan Empire.

_____ 8. The Pax Romana was a period of
  a. equal rights for all.
  b. direct democracy.
  c. expansion and civil war.
  d. peace and prosperity.

_____ 9. Christianity became popular as
  a. Augustus Caesar expanded the empire.
  b. science and the arts enriched the empire.
  c. Hellenistic culture made its way to Rome.
  d. violence and unrest created instability in Rome.

_____ 10. The Roman Empire fell because of
  a. the rise of Christianity.
  b. the death of Augustus Caesar.
  c. economic troubles and barbarian invasions.
  d. the rise of direct democracy.

Name _____ Class _____ Date _____

PROLOGUE

Daily Quiz P.4

Africa and the Americas

SHORT ANSWER Write a short answer for each of the following questions.

1. How were early African villages governed? _____
   _____

2. How did Christianity take hold in the Ethiopian highlands? _____
   _____

3. What brought Muslim influences to East Africa? _____
   _____

4. Which African kingdom was described as "seldom unjust?" _____
   _____

5. What maintained the wealth and power of West African kingdoms? _____
   _____

6. What affected the way native Americans built houses or found food? ____
   _____

7. Which early American culture had the only known form of writing? _____
   _____

8. How did the Aztecs worship their gods? _____
   _____

9. What was the basis of Inca religion? _____
   _____

10. How did the Incas try to prevent starvation in their empire? _____
    _____

ANSWER KEY

Chapter 1

DAILY QUIZ 1.1
Matching
1. h
2. l
3. d
4. g
5. k
6. b
7. c
8. a
9. e
10. i

DAILY QUIZ 1.2
True/False
1. F Agricultural settlements were able to produce and save their own food and develop civilizations.
2. T
3. T
4. F Artisans were skilled workers.
5. F It's called cultural diffusion.
6. T
7. T
8. F Iron is stronger than bronze.
9. F The plow gave men power over food production.
10. F People believed that gods and goddesses controlled their lives.

Chapter 2

DAILY QUIZ 2.1
Fill in the Blank
1. Nile
2. irrigation
3. desert and seas
4. hieroglyphics
5. Rosetta Stone
6. Old Kingdom
7. nobles
8. foreigners
9. Hatshepsut
10. monotheism

DAILY QUIZ 2.2
Multiple Choice
1. b
2. a
3. a
4. c
5. d
6. a
7. c
8. c
9. b
10. d

DAILY QUIZ 2.3
True/False
1. F The Fertile Crescent was open and easily reached by invaders.
2. T
3. F The Tigris and Euphrates flooded unpredictably.
4. F Sumerians created cuneiform writing.
5. F The arch can provide strong support for roofs.
6. T
7. F The Sumerians believed that the city-states belonged to the gods.
8. T
9. F Only upper-class males received an education.
10. T

DAILY QUIZ 2.4
Matching
1. d
2. l
3. e
4. i
5. a
6. c
7. h
8. j
9. k
10. g

DAILY QUIZ 2.5
Short Answer
1. The Lebanon mountains were hard to cross.
2. by sea
3. Carthage, Sicily, Sardinia, Malta, Spain
4. lumber
5. gold, silver, glass, dye, fish, linen, olive oil, wine
6. Egyptians and Babylonians
7. to exchange one good or service for another
8. the Phoenician alphabet
9. They used coined money.
10. a system that uses money as a measure of value and a unit of accounting

ANSWER KEY

DAILY QUIZ 2.6
Multiple Choice
1. a
2. c
3. c
4. b
5. d
6. c
7. a
8. b
9. b
10. a

Chapter 3

DAILY QUIZ 3.1
Matching
1. d
2. i
3. b
4. e
5. c
6. k
7. a
8. h
9. f
10. j

DAILY QUIZ 3.2
Multiple Choice
1. d
2. c
3. c
4. a
5. a
6. b
7. d
8. b
9. a
10. b

DAILY QUIZ 3.3
Matching
1. l
2. f
3. a
4. e
5. b
6. d
7. c
8. k
9. g
10. i

DAILY QUIZ 3.4
Fill in the Blank
1. invaders
2. the Magadha
3. Chandragupta Maurya
4. rigid bureaucracy
5. Aśoka
6. Buddhist
7. living conditions
8. fighting among Aśoka's sons
9. Hinduism
10. local leaders

DAILY QUIZ 3.5
True/False
1. T
2. T
3. F   The Hindu Laws of Manu required women to always obey men.
4. F   Suttee was the practice of widows committing suicide at their husbands' deaths.
5. F   The Panchatantra were fables from the Gupta period.
6. T
7. F   Aśoka was a Buddhist who encouraged the building of stupas.
8. F   Lower caste children were only allowed to study crafts and trade.
9. T
10. F Inoculations are a way of preventing disease.

Chapter 4

DAILY QUIZ 4.1
Fill in the Blank
1. rice
2. Proper
3. Manchuria, Mongolia, Tibet, Xinjiang, or northern Korea
4. loess, soil
5. Sorrow
6. Dikes
7. commercial waterways
8. deserts
9. identity, superiority
10. center of the world

DAILY QUIZ 4.2
Multiple Choice
1. b
2. a
3. d
4. d
5. c
6. c
7. b
8. a
9. b
10. b

ANSWER KEY

DAILY QUIZ 4.3
True/False
1. F The Zhou granted territories to members of their families and allies.
2. T
3. F The Qin established an autocracy, which gave the emperor absolute power.
4. F Cheng executed those who criticized the government.
5. F The Qin built walls along their borders.
6. T
7. F The Han dynasty extended its rule in all directions.
8. T
9. F Liu Ch'e created the leveling system to balance farm shortages and surpluses.
10. F The Han dynasty prospered because of trade along the Silk Road.

DAILY QUIZ 4.4
Matching
1. i
2. g
3. c
4. d
5. k
6. e
7. f
8. j
9. a
10. b

DAILY QUIZ 4.5
Fill in the Blank
1. family
2. individual
3. genealogy
4. ancestors
5. father
6. Qin dynasty
7. The Five Classics
8. The Book of Rites
9. seismograph
10. acupuncture

Chapter 5

DAILY QUIZ 5.1
True/False
1. F The Greek mainland is bordered by the Mediterranean, Aegean, and Ionian Seas.
2. F The geography of Greece isolated small villages.
3. T
4. F Tidal waves from a volcano eruption destroyed many Minoan villages.
5. T
6. F The Mycenaeans adopted many of the features of Minoan life.
7. F Polis means city-state.
8. T
9. F Only free males had rights.
10. T

DAILY QUIZ 5.2
Multiple Choice
1. b
2. a
3. c
4. a
5. a
6. b
7. d
8. c
9. c
10. d

DAILY QUIZ 5.3
Fill in the Blank
1. helots
2. political power
3. ephors
4. freedom
5. wealth
6. were born outside of Athens
7. archons
8. Solon
9. Cleisthenes
10. citizens participate in making decisions

ANSWER KEY

DAILY QUIZ 5.4
Short Answer
1. They set up colonies and traded goods in the Mediterranean.
2. They believed that money should be spent on buildings that benefited the public.
3. to have children
4. They could not own or inherit property. They were inferior to their husbands.
5. Sappho
6. a male slave who taught Athenian boys manners
7. Athenian boys were athletes as well as students.
8. wise
9. the study of what is good and what is bad
10. the study of public speaking and debate

DAILY QUIZ 5.5
Multiple Choice
1. b
2. a
3. a
4. c
5. d
6. d
7. d
8. a
9. b
10. c

Chapter 6

DAILY QUIZ 6.1
Fill in the Blank
1. golden age
2. beauty
3. Acropolis
4. Parthenon
5. everyday life
6. lifelike/natural/realistic
7. Zeus at the Temple of Olympia
8. human
9. city-state
10. harmony/order

DAILY QUIZ 6.2
Matching
1. j
2. m
3. c
4. d
5. g
6. k
7. a
8. n
9. e
10. b

DAILY QUIZ 6.3
Multiple Choice
1. a
2. d
3. d
4. b
5. c
6. a
7. c
8. c
9. a
10. d

DAILY QUIZ 6.4
True/False
1. F A middle class prospered during the Hellenistic Age.
2. T
3. T
4. F Members of other cultures began to regard themselves as Greek.
5. F Many people sought out new religions to help gain control of their lives.
6. F Cynicism was based on a disregard for wealth or status.
7. T
8. F Stoics believed that divine reason directs the world and that all people have some divinity in themselves.
9. T
10. F Hellenistic scientists such as Aristarchus began to believe the sun was the center of the universe.

Chapter 7

DAILY QUIZ 7.1
Fill in the Blank
1. Tiber
2. Etruscans
3. republic
4. Senate
5. praetors
6. Censors
7. checks and balances
8. tribunes
9. Plebeians
10. laws of Rome

ANSWER KEY

DAILY QUIZ 7.2
Multiple Choice
1. d
2. b
3. b
4. c
5. d
6. a
7. c
8. d
9. a
10. c

DAILY QUIZ 7.3
True/False
1. T
2. F The war for citizenship was the Social War.
3. F Private armies were more loyal to their generals than to Rome.
4. F Julius Caesar strengthened his power by making Egypt an ally.
5. T
6. F The Second Triumvirate consisted of Octavian, Marc Antony, and Lepidus.
7. T
8. T
9. F Nero is blamed for the fire that destroyed Rome.
10. F Marcus Aurelius preferred peace to war.

DAILY QUIZ 7.4
Short Answer
1. a strong government, trade and transportation, and a strong army
2. New laws were passed as needed. Old laws were interpreted to apply to a new world.
3. farming
4. They allowed Romans to transport goods and move armies quickly.
5. The army guarded the borders and kept peace in the provinces.
6. No, the rich were very rich, and the poor had almost nothing.
7. the father
8. aqueducts
9. They are all poets.
10. Latin

DAILY QUIZ 7.5
Matching
1. e
2. m
3. k
4. f
5. c
6. d
7. l
8. h
9. n
10. i

DAILY QUIZ 7.6
True/False
1. T
2. F Diocletian used a co-emperor and assistants to control the empire.
3. T
4. F The eastern part of the empire became stronger than the western empire.
5. T
6. F The Huns attacked Gaul, but were defeated by Rome.
7. F The tribes were not unified and destroyed much of Roman history while fighting.
8. F The eastern part survived into the 1400s.
9. T
10. T

Chapter 8

DAILY QUIZ 8.1
Short Answer
1. They protected against invaders. Rapids made communication and trade between villages difficult.
2. It used to be fertile and well-watered; now it is dry and barren.
3. Savannas are dry grasslands.
4. areas of dense plants that have access to sunlight
5. The hot wet climate provides a breeding ground for disease-carrying insects.
6. a group of ancient African languages
7. speakers and entertainers who learned the oral traditions of their village
8. that Africans had contact with Asia
9. Women were the primary farmers. People traced their ancestry and inherited property through their mothers.
10. the village elders

ANSWER KEY

DAILY QUIZ 8.2
Multiple Choice
1. b
2. a
3. d
4. b
5. a
6. b
7. c
8. d
9. c
10. a

DAILY QUIZ 8.3
True/False
1. F The monsoon winds helped to link the ports on the Indian Ocean.
2. T
3. F They helped to create the Swahili culture.
4. F Kilwa was the leading port city on the East African coast.
5. T
6. F Great Zimbabwe may have declined because of overpopulation.
7. T
8. T
9. T
10. F Moroccan invaders helped to bring down the Songhai Empire.

Chapter 9

DAILY QUIZ 9.1
Fill in the Blank
1. Andes Mountains
2. Amazon
3. strait
4. Asia
5. climate changes, following herds
6. how the world was formed and how people came into being
7. hunter-gatherers
8. many large animals became extinct
9. horses to pull them
10. form permanent settlements

DAILY QUIZ 9.2
True/False
1. F They survived by fishing.
2. F They were a way to tell about a community's history.
3. T
4. T
5. F The Hohokam used irrigation to farm in the dry southwestern climate.
6. F The Pueblo used adobe to build.
7. T
8. F Buffalo were sacred, not dogs.
9. F They probably used the earthen mounds for burial or for ceremonies.
10. T

DAILY QUIZ 9.3
Short Answer
1. the Olmec
2. Yes, they wrote with hieroglyphs.
3. They created an accurate agricultural calendar.
4. a god worshipped by the Toltec and later by other cultures
5. the Aztec
6. the military
7. human sacrifice
8. discontent among the people forced to pay heavy tribute to the Aztec
9. children of the sun
10. They built roads, used a common language, and had an educational system.

Chapter 10 (Modern Chapter 1)

DAILY QUIZ 10.1
Multiple Choice
1. c
2. d
3. a
4. a
5. c
6. d
7. b
8. c
9. c
10. a

ANSWER KEY

DAILY QUIZ 10.2
Fill in the Blank
1. steppe
2. rivers
3. Slavs
4. trade routes
5. Rurik
6. boyars
7. veche
8. code of laws
9. Vladimir I
10. taiga

DAILY QUIZ 10.3
True/False
1. F Kievan Russia declined due to political infighting and loss of trade.
2. F Mongol invaders conquered almost all of Kievan Russia.
3. T
4. T
5. F Prince Ivan I gained power by cooperating with Mongol leaders.
6. T
7. F Ivan the Terrible ruled with absolute power.
8. F Russia grew in size and power under Ivan's rule.
9. T
10. F Moscow became the center of the church after Turks conquered Constantinople.

Chapter 11 (Modern Chapter 2)

DAILY QUIZ 11.1
Matching
1. g
2. i
3. a
4. c
5. e
6. h
7. f
8. j
9. b
10. k

DAILY QUIZ 11.2
Multiple Choice
1. c
2. a
3. b
4. a
5. a
6. a
7. c
8. a
9. b
10. a

DAILY QUIZ 11.3
Fill in the Blank
1. trade
2. caliphates
3. Qu'ran
4. slaves
5. divorced
6. Córdoba
7. astrolabe
8. algebra
9. to show God or the human or animal form
10. Scheherazade

Chapter 12 (Modern Chapter 3)

DAILY QUIZ 12.1
True/False
1. T
2. F The Tang dynasty extended China's frontiers, allowing influence from Korea, Japan, and India.
3. T
4. F Du Fu wrote poetry about the hardships of war.
5. F Empress Wu supported Buddhism.
6. T
7. F The Tang dynasty destroyed the Buddhist monasteries.
8. F The Sung had to pay tribute to the Mongols to avoid war.
9. T
10. T

ANSWER KEY

DAILY QUIZ 12.2
Multiple Choice
1. a
2. b
3. a
4. c
5. b
6. c
7. a
8. d
9. a
10. b

DAILY QUIZ 12.3
Fill in the Blank
1. islands
2. Shinto
3. *The Tale of Genji*
4. shogun
5. samurai
6. Zen Buddhism
7. Yi Dynasty
8. nobles/aristocrats
9. Mahayana Buddhism
10. Khmer

Chapter 13 (Modern Chapter 4)

DAILY QUIZ 13.1
Matching
1. d
2. l
3. i
4. a
5. f
6. b
7. e
8. c
9. j
10. h

DAILY QUIZ 13.2
Multiple Choice
1. b
2. a
3. d
4. d
5. c
6. d
7. c
8. b
9. a
10. d

DAILY QUIZ 13.3
True/False
1. T
2. F The church gained power because of weak central governments in Europe.
3. F Parish priests were the lowest ranked members of the church.
4. T
5. F The pope's most important advisors were the cardinals.
6. T
7. F The church punished a region by issuing an interdict.
8. T
9. F Tithes were the money paid by the parishoners to the church.
10. F Simony was the practice of paying for a high church position.

DAILY QUIZ 13.4
Fill in the Blank
1. shires
2. William of Normandy
3. king
4. Thomas Becket
5. Magna Carta
6. Parliament
7. common law
8. Capetian
9. Estates General
10. unified

DAILY QUIZ 13.5
Short Answer
1. because he had helped defend the pope from the Roman nobles
2. Germany and northern Italy
3. Henry III
4. Gregory VII
5. whether or not the emperor had the right to appoint bishops
6. The pope revoked Henry IV's excommunication.
7. Concordat of Worms
8. take control of Italy
9. Lombard League
10. Innocent III

ANSWER KEY

Chapter 14 (Modern Chapter 5)

DAILY QUIZ 14.1
Multiple Choice
1. c
2. a
3. b
4. d
5. c
6. d
7. c
8. d
9. b
10. c

DAILY QUIZ 14.2
True/False
1. F It decreased trade because everything was made in one location.
2. T
3. F Viking traders generally brought things north.
4. F German cities formed the Hanseatic League.
5. T
6. F Traders paid taxes to local officials for each item sold at the fairs.
7. T
8. F The domestic system means that all work is done from the home.
9. T
10. F A market economy means that business is controlled by individuals.

DAILY QUIZ 14.3
Fill in the Blank
1. rights
2. Exemption
3. Commercial privileges
4. Merchant guilds
5. Craft guilds
6. apprentice
7. journeyman
8. kings
9. The plague or Black Death
10. higher wages

DAILY QUIZ 14.4
Matching
1. f
2. i
3. d
4. g
5. c
6. a
7. j
8. e
9. h
10. b

DAILY QUIZ 14.5
Multiple Choice
1. d
2. a
3. c
4. b
5. a
6. c
7. a
8. a
9. b
10. d

DAILY QUIZ 14.6
True/False
1. F They believed that the church interfered too much.
2. T
3. F Boniface fought back when Philip IV decreed the clergy should pay taxes.
4. T
5. F It refers to the years when French kings controlled the popes in Avignon.
6. F The Great Schism is the years when France and Rome supported different popes.
7. T
8. F It said the pope should not have control over worldly rulers.
9. T
10. F Jan Hus was executed.

Chapter 15 (Modern Chapter 6)

DAILY QUIZ 15.1
Matching
1. a
2. j
3. d
4. h
5. b
6. e
7. c
8. g
9. f
10. i

ANSWER KEY

DAILY QUIZ 15.2
Multiple Choice
1. c
2. a
3. a
4. b
5. d
6. b
7. b
8. a
9. d
10. c

DAILY QUIZ 15.3
True/False
1. F Weak princes allowed for independent ideas about religion.
2. T
3. F The 95 Theses protested the selling of indulgences.
4. F Lutherans believed that Christians could interpret the Bible themselves.
5. F The Peace of Augsburg gave each German ruler the right to choose religion.
6. F Henry VIII broke away from the Catholic Church and named himself head of the new church in order to obtain a divorce.
7. T
8. T
9. T
10. T

DAILY QUIZ 15.4
Fill in the Blank
1. Counter-Reformation
2. Inquisition
3. *Index of Forbidden Books*
4. Council of Trent
5. Catholic
6. Jesuits
7. education
8. humanism
9. other beliefs
10. increase

DAILY QUIZ 15.5
Multiple Choice
1. c
2. b
3. d
4. a
5. a
6. d
7. b
8. b
9. a
10. c

Chapter 16 (Modern Chapter 7)

DAILY QUIZ 16.1
True/False
1. F Natural philosophers used religious teachings and classical thought to explain nature.
2. T
3. F Copernicus introduced the idea of the heliocentric universe.
4. F Kepler helped confirm Copernicus' theories.
5. F Galileo proved wrong Aristotle's belief that heavier objects fall faster than lighter ones.
6. T
7. F They made contributions to the study of anatomy.
8. T
9. F Bacon believed truths had to be demonstrated physically, rather than discovered using reasoning and logic.
10. T

DAILY QUIZ 16.2
Fill in the Blank
1. sea routes
2. compass
3. Commercial Revolution
4. standard values/fixed values
5. joint-stock
6. mercantilism
7. exported more goods than it took in
8. tariff
9. subsidies
10. religious or political persecution

ANSWER KEY

DAILY QUIZ 16.3
Matching
1. g
2. b
3. k
4. a
5. d
6. h
7. c
8. i
9. e
10. l

DAILY QUIZ 16.4
Multiple Choice
1. b
2. d
3. d
4. a
5. b
6. b
7. a
8. a
9. b
10. c

Chapter 17 (Modern Chapter 8)

DAILY QUIZ 17.1
Fill in the Blank
1. junks
2. self-sufficient
3. defense
4. scholars
5. Manchuria
6. queues
7. merchants
8. philology
9. corruption
10. White Lotus Rebellion

DAILY QUIZ 17.2
Multiple Choice
1. c
2. c
3. a
4. b
5. d
6. b
7. a
8. d
9. c
10. d

DAILY QUIZ 17.3
True/False
1. F He defeated the last of the Ashikaga shoguns.
2. F Hideyoshi attempted to conquer Korea, but his death stopped their advance.
3. F His government was a combination of a monarchy and feudalism.
4. F The Tokugawa shoguns forced daimyo to live in Edo every other year and kept the daimyo's families hostage in Edo.
5. F Some shunned muskets as against their tradition of fighting.
6. T
7. F Warriors were the most important.
8. F Perry offered a treaty to Japan, then let the shogunate think about it for a year.
9. F After Japan opened more ports to the United States, other nations gained trade access.
10. T

Chapter 18 (Modern Chapter 9)

DAILY QUIZ 18.1
Matching
1. h
2. e
3. a
4. b
5. d
6. j
7. c
8. f
9. g
10. i

DAILY QUIZ 18.2
Multiple Choice
1. b
2. c
3. d
4. a
5. a
6. d
7. a
8. b
9. b
10. c

ANSWER KEY

DAILY QUIZ 18.3
Fill in the Blank
1. Rajputs
2. Babur
3. tax
4. Urdu
5. tolerated
6. divine ruler
7. Hall of Private Audience
8. power
9. Islamic/Muslim
10. religions

Chapter 19 (Modern Chapter 10)

DAILY QUIZ 19.1
Multiple Choice
1. b
2. a
3. d
4. c
5. a
6. a
7. b
8. a
9. a
10. b

DAILY QUIZ 19.2
True/False
1. T
2. F Peter the Great went to the West himself.
3. F Peter wanted to be closer to the West.
4. T
5. F It meant that lands and serfs were awarded on the basis of service to Peter.
6. F Peter made the nobles more dependent on him.
7. F Catherine supported the arts for her benefit as well as the nobles'.
8. F Catherine's efforts were successful.
9. T
10. T

DAILY QUIZ 19.3
Fill in the Blank
1. Pragmatic Sanction
2. Brandenburg-Prussia
3. Great Elector
4. King of Prussia
5. Louis XIV
6. military
7. Prussian
8. Austria
9. North America
10. withdraw

DAILY QUIZ 19.4
Matching
1. g
2. e
3. c
4. b
5. d
6. a
7. h
8. j
9. l
10. i

Chapter 20 (Modern Chapter 11)

DAILY QUIZ 20.1
Fill in the Blank
1. Petition of Right
2. dismiss Parliament
3. Long Parliament
4. civil war
5. Roundheads
6. Oliver Cromwell
7. commonwealth
8. military dictator
9. constitution
10. Navigation Act of 1651

DAILY QUIZ 20.2
Matching
1. c
2. a
3. f
4. j
5. d
6. b
7. h
8. i
9. g
10. k

ANSWER KEY

DAILY QUIZ 20.3
Multiple Choice
1. a
2. d
3. a
4. a
5. d
6. b
7. c
8. a
9. d
10. a

DAILY QUIZ 20.4
True/False
1. F The 18th century is the Age of Enlightenment.
2. T
3. T
4. F It was a collection of technical and critical articles about many subjects.
5. F He argued for a government that provided checks and balances.
6. T
7. F Rousseau believed that people were naturally good and did not need strong government.
8. F It is a government created and controlled by the people.
9. F It is rule by an absolute monarch who is guided by the principles of the Enlightenment.
10. T

DAILY QUIZ 20.5
Fill in the Blank
1. Stamp Act
2. Loyalists
3. Second Continental Congress
4. people
5. cross the ocean, transport supplies and equipment
6. unity
7. Benjamin Franklin
8. states
9. federal system
10. individuals

Chapter 21 (Modern Chapter 12)

DAILY QUIZ 21.1
True/False
1. T
2. F It meant the clergy of the Roman Catholic Church.
3. F The Third Estate meant the middle class, such as merchants and professionals.
4. T
5. F Both classes were unhappy.
6. F She was Austrian.
7. F Louis XV was peaceful, but inherited debt and increased it because of his lavish lifestyle.
8. T
9. F The Third Estate demanded that each member be given an individual vote.
10. F The Third Estate refused to meet separately and cast one vote. The Third Estate then asked the other two estates to join it in writing a constitution.

DAILY QUIZ 21.2
Multiple Choice
1. b
2. a
3. c
4. a
5. d
6. b
7. c
8. a
9. a
10. d

DAILY QUIZ 21.3
Matching
1. i
2. d
3. e
4. a
5. c
6. k
7. f
8. g
9. h
10. l

ANSWER KEY

DAILY QUIZ 24.3
Matching
1. d
2. i
3. f
4. a
5. h
6. g
7. b
8. l
9. k
10. j

DAILY QUIZ 24.4
True/False
1. F The colonies were only allowed to trade with Spain or Portugal.
2. F They were large estates that were given to privileged friends of the empire.
3. T
4. F Creoles were white people born in the colonies.
5. F They revolted against French settlers to gain freedom for Haiti.
6. F Miguel Hidalgo y Costilla led the revolt.
7. T
8. T
9. F The creoles were conservative, and the mestizos were liberal.
10. T

Chapter 25 (Modern Chapter 16)

DAILY QUIZ 25.1
Fill in the Blank
1. risorgimento
2. Carbonari
3. republic
4. Young Italy Movement
5. the pope
6. Cavour
7. Napoléon III
8. the kingdom of Sardinia
9. Garibaldi
10. Victor Emmanuel II

DAILY QUIZ 25.2
Multiple Choice
1. b
2. a
3. a
4. b
5. b
6. d
7. a
8. d
9. d
10. a

DAILY QUIZ 25.3
True/False
1. F Upper-class conservatives and other regions of Germany were threats.
2. T
3. F It was an anti-Catholic program.
4. T
5. F Cartels were a way for the German economy to gain strength.
6. F They encouraged government ownership.
7. F The laws had little effect.
8. T
9. F He believed in an absolute monarchy.
10. F William II forced Bismarck to resign.

DAILY QUIZ 25.4
Matching
1. c
2. h
3. f
4. b
5. e
6. d
7. a
8. j
9. k
10. g

DAILY QUIZ 25.5
Multiple Choice
1. a
2. d
3. a
4. c
5. d
6. a
7. b
8. d
9. d
10. a

ANSWER KEY

Chapter 26 (Modern Chapter 17)

DAILY QUIZ 26.1
True/False
1. T
2. F Many empires had roots in trade and economic opportunity as well.
3. F A settlement colony is a large group of people from one area living in a new place.
4. T
5. F Nationalist feeling made countries want to increase their power.
6. F Imperialist nations created hatred among colonized people.
7. F Industrialism forced empires to seek more colonies for raw materials and markets.
8. T
9. F European countries tried to Westernize their colonies.
10. F Missionaries helped teach and provide medical care.

DAILY QUIZ 26.2
Multiple Choice
1. c
2. b
3. a
4. b
5. a
6. d
7. b
8. a
9. c
10. d

DAILY QUIZ 26.3
Matching
1. a
2. f
3. b
4. g
5. c
6. i
7. k
8. d
9. l
10. e

DAILY QUIZ 26.4
True/False
1. T
2. F British and Indian society rarely mixed.
3. T
4. T
5. F The Meiji Restoration led to a relaxation in the social system.
6. T
7. F The war was fought over Korean independence.
8. T
9. F The British withdrew from the Samoa Islands because of its involvement in the Boer War.
10. T

DAILY QUIZ 26.5
Multiple Choice
1. c
2. b
3. a
4. a
5. c
6. a
7. d
8. c
9. b
10. d

Chapter 27 (Modern Chapter 18)

DAILY QUIZ 27.1
True/False
1. T
2. F Nationalism led to militarism and increased military building.
3. F It was an effort to isolate France.
4. F It was a fear of Germany, not Russia. Russia was part of the Triple Entente.
5. T
6. F Britain and Russia's alliance was strengthened by their mutual fear of German expansion.
7. F Austria-Hungary feared Russia's support of the Serbs.
8. F Austria-Hungary declared war after Serbia could not agree on the last term of the ultimatum.
9. T
10. F Germany ignored Belgium's declaration of neutrality.

ANSWER KEY

DAILY QUIZ 27.2
Multiple Choice
1. c
2. b
3. a
4. b
5. a
6. c
7. b
8. c
9. a
10. d

DAILY QUIZ 27.3
Fill in the Blank
1. inadequate
2. dissolved
3. army
4. council
5. economic equality
6. continue
7. Communist Party
8. signing a treaty with the Central Powers
9. Red Army
10. the Union of Soviet Socialist Republics, or the Soviet Union

DAILY QUIZ 27.4
Multiple Choice
1. d
2. c
3. c
4. b
5. d
6. a
7. a
8. a
9. d
10. d

DAILY QUIZ 27.5
True/False
1. T
2. F It punished Germany.
3. F Germany had to pay all reparations.
4. T
5. F Germany was required to disarm, but the Allies did not have the ability to enforce this requirement.
6. F Yugoslavia was made up of Balkan states.
7. T
8. F It had a council, not a world bank.
9. F The League would hold colonies in trust until they were "ready for independence."
10. F Americans feared being dragged into wars over issues that did not directly concern them.

Chapter 28 (Modern Chapter 19)

DAILY QUIZ 28.1
Matching
1. d
2. g
3. k
4. h
5. f
6. l
7. e
8. i
9. j
10. a

DAILY QUIZ 28.2
Fill in the Blank
1. a decline/depression, debt
2. protect domestic industry
3. High tariffs
4. market speculation
5. overvalued/inflated
6. stock market crash
7. industrialized
8. social programs
9. New Deal
10. Social Security Act

DAILY QUIZ 28.3
Multiple Choice
1. a
2. c
3. d
4. b
5. a
6. a
7. a
8. d
9. c
10. a

DAILY QUIZ 28.4
True/False
1. F He developed the fascist party.
2. F Those values appeal to the upper classes.
3. T
4. F He appealed to anti-communist feeling.
5. T
6. T
7. F Hitler was an anti-communist.
8. F He promised to rebuild the military.
9. F It meant that they would eliminate everyone but "pure" Germans.
10. F France and Britain didn't think it was worth potential war.

ANSWER KEY

DAILY QUIZ 28.5
Fill in the Blank
1. War Communism
2. free enterprise
3. Collective farming
4. revolution
5. Stalin
6. Command Economy
7. agriculture
8. Politburo
9. purge
10. encourage worldwide Communist revolution

Chapter 29 (Modern Chapter 20)

DAILY QUIZ 29.1
Multiple Choice
1. b
2. a
3. d
4. b
5. c
6. b
7. c
8. a
9. c
10. c

DAILY QUIZ 29.2
True/False
1. F Greek troops went to Turkey to impose the terms of the peace treaty.
2. F Kemal installed a one-party system.
3. T
4. F Kemal believed that Turkey's survival depended on Westernization.
5. F Under Kemal, Turkey became prosperous and independent.
6. T
7. T
8. F Iran sought a closer alliance with Germany.
9. F Western education led Africans to seek similar independence.
10. T

DAILY QUIZ 29.3
Fill in the Blank
1. Open Door Policy
2. modernization
3. anti-foreigner
4. Kuomintang
5. industrialize
6. an end to foreign influence
7. the Soviet Union
8. Chiang Kai-shek
9. communists
10. peasants

DAILY QUIZ 29.4
Multiple Choice
1. d
2. b
3. b
4. c
5. c
6. c
7. c
8. b
9. d
10. a

DAILY QUIZ 29.5
True/False
1. F They were owned primarily by British and American companies.
2. F Foreign investment helped build power sources.
3. T
4. F A growing middle class added to political dissent.
5. F Rivera was an artist who painted about working-class concerns.
6. F Latin American exports were severely hit by the Great Depression.
7. T
8. F It called for nonintervention in Latin American affairs.
9. T
10. F Mexico's nationalizing of the oil industry helped it become independent.

Chapter 30 (Modern Chapter 21)

DAILY QUIZ 30.1
Fill in the Blank
1. illegal
2. fascist
3. Manchuria
4. Ethiopia
5. Economic sanctions
6. Falange
7. Loyalists
8. fascist
9. International Brigade
10. military dictatorship

ANSWER KEY

DAILY QUIZ 30.2
Multiple Choice
1. b
2. d
3. c
4. b
5. a
6. c
7. a
8. c
9. c
10. c

DAILY QUIZ 30.3
Matching
1. f
2. j
3. g
4. b
5. a
6. l
7. i
8. k
9. e
10. c

DAILY QUIZ 30.4
True/False
1. F Spain remained neutral, but let Germany use its ports.
2. T
3. F They were beaten back by the Allies.
4. F Germany invaded the Soviet Union without officially declaring war.
5. F The United States and Britain offered aid to the Soviets.
6. T
7. F Japan continued to attack China.
8. F The United States gave aid to Chinese nationalists and placed an embargo on the sale of oil and scrap iron to Japan. The United States also protested violations of the Nine-Power Pact of 1922.
9. T
10. F Japan invaded the Philippines.

DAILY QUIZ 30.5
Multiple Choice
1. c
2. a
3. b
4. c
5. d
6. b
7. a
8. b
9. a
10. b

DAILY QUIZ 30.6
Fill in the Blank
1. Stalingrad
2. North Africa
3. "soft underbelly of the Axis"
4. Fascist Party
5. Australia
6. skip others
7. Operation Overlord
8. Victory in Europe
9. Yalta
10. the bombing of Hiroshima and Nagasaki

Chapter 31 (Modern Chapter 22)

DAILY QUIZ 31.1
True/False
1. F They agreed these countries should have their own elections to determine their futures.
2. T
3. F Roosevelt proposed it.
4. F They agreed that Germany would be only temporarily divided.
5. F They wanted Germany to remain industrialized to help Europe's economy.
6. F They declared it a criminal organization.
7. F The General Assembly was open to all.
8. F They voted for republics.
9. F They wanted communist governments.
10. T

DAILY QUIZ 31.2
Multiple Choice
1. a
2. a
3. c
4. d
5. b
6. d
7. b
8. a
9. d
10. c

ANSWER KEY

DAILY QUIZ 31.3
Fill in the Blank
1. market
2. Social Democrats
3. Berlin Wall
4. welfare state
5. Algerian independence
6. presidency
7. The EEC
8. Nikita Khrushchev
9. collectivized
10. Hungary, Czechoslovakia, East Germany

DAILY QUIZ 31.4
Matching
1. a
2. e
3. f
4. c
5. i
6. b
7. d
8. h
9. g
10. l

Chapter 32 (Modern Chapter 23)

DAILY QUIZ 32.1
Multiple Choice
1. b
2. d
3. c
4. c
5. a
6. d
7. a
8. a
9. a
10. c

DAILY QUIZ 32.2
True/False
1. T
2. F — Chiang Kai-shek formed a government on Taiwan. Mao Zedong formed the People's Republic of China.
3. F — Industrial output decreased, and food shortages became common.
4. T
5. T
6. F — Deng Xiaoping began to open China to the West.
7. F — The Tiananmen Square Massacre was the result of a call for democracy.
8. T
9. F — South Korea's economy grew while North Korea's worsened.
10. F — China considers Taiwan a province, not an independent nation.

DAILY QUIZ 32.3
Fill in the Blank
1. demilitarize
2. parliamentary democracy
3. war
4. zaibatsu
5. technology
6. family
7. militarism
8. military
9. Kuril Islands
10. Liberal-Democratic Party

DAILY QUIZ 32.4
Matching
1. d
2. e
3. b
4. f
5. c
6. a
7. l
8. h
9. k
10. j

DAILY QUIZ 32.5
Multiple Choice
1. a
2. b
3. b
4. a
5. a
6. a
7. b
8. b
9. a
10. c

Chapter 33 (Modern Chapter 24)

DAILY QUIZ 33.1
Matching
1. b
2. h
3. c
4. e
5. a
6. i
7. k
8. g
9. d
10. f

DAILY QUIZ 33.2
True/False
1. F — Nkrumah used a strong economy to seize power.
2. T
3. F — Biafra surrendered to Nigeria.
4. F — Ethnic fighting between the Tutsi and Hutu erupted into widespread slaughter.
5. F — Zaire let the Hutu expel the Tutsi.

ANSWER KEY

6. T
7. F Dependence on one product easily led to sudden economic declines.
8. F Reduced competition between superpowers lessened the press for civil war.
9. F The UN failed to calm the fighting.
10. T

DAILY QUIZ 33.3
Fill in the Blank
1. *colons*
2. freed Algiers
3. Arab state
4. a Jewish state and Arab state
5. Israel
6. Suez Crisis
7. dictatorship
8. Egypt
9. Iran
10. civilian

DAILY QUIZ 33.4
Multiple Choice
1. c
2. d
3. a
4. a
5. d
6. d
7. a
8. b
9. c
10. d

Chapter 34 (Modern Chapter 25)

DAILY QUIZ 34.1
True/False
1. F The profits usually did not stay in the host country.
2. F It means reliance on one crop.
3. T
4. T
5. F It was a trade agreement.
6. F It created a free trade zone for Mexico, the United States, and Canada.
7. F It grew rapidly.
8. T
9. F It's a group of women who oppose abuses of government and military power.
10. F It's a trade and defense group.

DAILY QUIZ 34.2
Matching
1. c
2. h
3. k
4. d
5. b
6. l
7. g
8. a
9. i
10. j

DAILY QUIZ 34.3
Multiple Choice
1. c
2. c
3. a
4. c
5. c
6. c
7. a
8. b
9. d
10. b

DAILY QUIZ 34.4
Fill in the Blank
1. foreign debt
2. lower-class workers and middle class
3. his wife, Eva Perón
4. disappeared people
5. Falkland Islands
6. Shining Path
7. cocaine
8. drug trade
9. U.S.
10. human rights

Chapter 35 (Modern Chapter 26)

DAILY QUIZ 35.1
Matching
1. e
2. g
3. d
4. h
5. a
6. c
7. i
8. f
9. b
10. k

DAILY QUIZ 35.2
Multiple Choice
1. a
2. b
3. a
4. b
5. a
6. c
7. c
8. d
9. c
10. a

ANSWER KEY

DAILY QUIZ 35.3
Fill in the Blank
1. moved away from communism
2. Afghanistan
3. glasnost, perestroika
4. Boris Yeltsin
5. organized crime
6. Chechnya
7. Poland
8. Czechoslovakia
9. religions
10. Dayton Accord

DAILY QUIZ 35.4
True/False
1. T
2. F   The terrorist attacks included the World Trade Center in New York City, the Pentagon near Washington, D.C., and a hijacked plane that crashed in Pennsylvania before reaching its target.
3. F   Few survivors were rescued from the site.
4. T
5. T
6. T
7. F   Congress passed a $40 billion relief package and passed legislation to provide compensation for victims' families.
8. F   More than 300 firefighters and many other rescue workers died at the World Trade Center.
9. T
10. T

Chapter 36 (Modern Chapter 27)

DAILY QUIZ 36.1
Matching
1. f
2. c
3. d
4. b
5. h
6. m
7. i
8. l
9. a
10. j

DAILY QUIZ 36.2
Multiple Choice
1. d
2. b
3. c
4. b
5. b
6. d
7. c
8. b
9. a
10. b

DAILY QUIZ 36.3
Fill in the Blank
1. UN
2. national sovereignty
3. human rights abuses
4. Amnesty International
5. community
6. GDP
7. dictatorships
8. pro-democracy
9. Soviet Union
10. Burma/Myanmar

Epilogue

DAILY QUIZ E.1
Multiple Choice
1. b
2. b
3. a
4. d
5. c
6. a
7. a
8. b
9. c
10. d

DAILY QUIZ E.2
True/False
1. F   Empires formed alliances to increase their strength.
2. F   Serbian anger led to World War I.
3. T
4. F   Economic hardship led to the Russian Revolution.
5. F   The Treaty sought to weaken and punish Germany.
6. F   The United States emerged economically stronger from World War I.
7. T
8. T
9. F   Asian countries felt that too much western influence had weakened them.
10. F   The Axis powers started the series of invasions that led to World War II.

ANSWER KEY

DAILY QUIZ E.3
Matching
1. h
2. l
3. i
4. k
5. a
6. f
7. b
8. d
9. e
10. j

DAILY QUIZ E.4
Fill in the Blank
1. exports
2. Great Leap Forward
3. Cultural Revolution
4. the Philippines
5. Vietnam
6. Pakistan
7. Benazir Bhutto
8. apartheid
9. Palestine
10. Camp David Accords

DAILY QUIZ E.5
Matching
1. k
2. d
3. i
4. a
5. j
6. b
7. c
8. g
9. e
10. h

DAILY QUIZ E.6
True/False
1. T
2. F The Pentagon was hit, and another plane with an unknown target was downed.
3. F Hundreds of doctors were standing by but, unfortunately, there were few survivors.
4. T
5. T
6. T
7. F The economy was not completely destroyed, and small gains were made.
8. F Close to 3,000 people were killed.
9. F The American people banded together as American citizens.
10. T

Prologue

DAILY QUIZ P.1
Fill in the Blank
1. Ice Age
2. New Stone Age
3. division of labor
4. Nile River
5. geometry
6. Amenhotep IV
7. city-states
8. Hammurabi
9. different kings
10. Torah

DAILY QUIZ P.2
True/False
1. F Warriors and then priests were the most important.
2. T
3. F Right views are part of the Eightfold Path.
4. T
5. F Chinese civilizations were isolated from most other peoples because of geographical features.
6. T
7. F Animism is the belief that spirits live in everything.
8. F The Qin dynasty fell because it was harsh and cruel.
9. T
10. F Confucian rules called for a gentle way of living based on respect.

DAILY QUIZ P.3
Multiple Choice
1. c
2. a
3. b
4. d
5. c
6. c
7. a
8. d
9. d
10. c

ANSWER KEY

DAILY QUIZ P.4
Short Answer
1. by the village elders
2. King ʿEzānā of Aksum became a Christian.
3. commercial opportunities
4. Mali
5. control of trade routes in the Sahara
6. the geography of the region
7. the Maya
8. human sacrifice
9. worship of the sun and moon
10. They stored food and distributed it when crops failed.